A **Navigating Reality™** Discovery-Guide Series

THE
JOB
DISCOVERY
TOOLBOX
GUIDE

*Expanding Your Work Options
From Job Search and
Career Planning to Employment*

An Interactive Discovery-Guide Navigating You Through
Useful Labor Market Information Websites
to Expand Your Options for Employment

Meryl Tsukiji
Developed in Collaboration with Joseph Holmes
Art Illustrations by Claire Fant

Collective Concerns Publications
Seattle, Washington

https://www.navigatingreality.com (learning tools and related information)
https://www.cconcerns.com (perspective-thinking concepts)
Contact: nr@navigatingreality.com

ISBN: 979-8-9890466-0-7 (Version A - Paperback)

ISBN: 979-8-9890466-1-4 (Version B - Digital PDF)

Library of Congress Control Number: 2023919479

Printed in the United States of America

Collective Concerns Publications
Seattle, Washington
Contact: nr@navigatingreality.com

Important note about The Job Discovery Toolbox Guide updates: The Department of Labor websites introduced in this Discovery-Guide are periodically updated. When major updates occur, a new edition of this Discovery-Guide will be published. However, for episodic and minor visual changes, information about website updates can be found at https://www. navigatingreality.com: Select "Learning Tools" and then "Discovery-Guide Updates" in the drop-down menu. If you notice updates before we do, please contact us at nr@navigatingreality.com. Thank you!

Design: Claire Fant
Possibilities Landscape Bridge, Happy Orange,
Happy Apple Tour Guide Art Illustrations by Claire Fant
Happy Apple Tour Guide inspired by Yuuki Hennessy's Happy Apple Art

A note to readers in terms of formatting: In consideration of both individuals and workshop groups, the AP and European style formatting has been mostly applied, such as in the use of serial commas and commas outside quotation marks, as well as the conventional use of numbers when referring to data, for ease when reading aloud in a group, as well as when reading to oneself.

In Celebration of Joseph Holmes
1956 - 2024

This Discovery-Guide is in recognition of Joseph Holmes for his dedicated, life-long career as a skilled and effective job counselor helping people find work, in jobs they want to have. Joseph's gentle soul, positive inspiration, and amazing sense of humor has touched many lives, including ours, and will now touch yours as well!

Joseph enthusiastically supported the importance of having a job search and career planning strategy. He wholeheartedly believed in the usefulness of using Labor Market Information (LMI) to help people find sustainable and meaningful work. Whenever he had the time, Joseph would animatedly explore and research many different Labor Market Information tools and platforms, like a kid in a candy store, full of only the best goodies.

Joseph loved his StreetStrider exercise outings.

This Discovery-Guide was developed and cultivated through in-person workshop trials and individual working sessions to include Joseph's 30+ years of seeing what worked, what helped, and what inspired people to find their best job fit. Joseph strongly believed in the strategic value offered throughout this Discovery-Guide and was incredibly enthusiastic about bringing our vision to life, and sharing this with you.

In honor of Joseph's commitment to improving the lives of others, we are dedicating this updated version, and future editions, in his memory. Joseph's patient nature, lively expressiveness and thoughtful expertise was a rarity to witness and enjoy. We hope you will glean a little of Joseph's positivity and hopefulness, as you work through this Discovery-Guide.

Table of Contents

WELCOME TO THE JOB DISCOVERY TOOLBOX!

I. A BRIEF INTRODUCTION

This Discovery-Guide is designed to help expand your work search options and enhance your ability to discover the work you find meaningful. Given the Covid-19 pandemic of 2020-2021+ (when so many of us lost work through no fault of our own), the workplace landscape has been changing at a faster pace than ever before. For example, our reliance on automation, robotics and artificial intelligence to replace traditional jobs is expected to occur more quickly now, and into the future. In addition, the way we find products and services, such as through online websites, will continue to impact available jobs. However, changes such as these create different and new opportunities as well. This Discovery-Guide is intended to help you find those new opportunities and identify different areas to look for work (occupational categories) based on YOUR interests and skills, and by adding your own innovative, creative thinking into this experience as well.

Looking forward, one major shift in jobs across our nation and the world involves less reliance on the historical use of land, labor and capital (such as with past lumber and manufacturing jobs) and more towards an emphasis on ideas. Often described as transitioning towards a creative economy (Howkins, J, 2001. *The Creative Economy*. London – Penguin Books.), this means your ingenuity, imagination, innovative ideas and creative interests will have a more important place in the future. Beginning now, employers are more than ever, looking for workers with an interest and curiosity to continuously improve their knowledge, skills and abilities. Your commitment to learning, improving and finding your own passion in the work you do, will help us usher in a new and improved future. Together, we can invest our efforts to find value in the work we do and by doing so, we can also support the best of our humanity. Finding meaning and enjoyment from the work you do will make a positive difference for us all!

Our Recommendation: As you work through this Discovery-Guide, the best approach is to continue through to the end, and not jump into applying for jobs before finishing. This way, you will have a more complete, actionable perspective with lots of different ideas, as well as "sets of tools" to expand your options, opportunities, and inspire your efforts.

We hope this Discovery-Guide serves as a useful tool in your job search activity for you to sustain, discover or re-discover, a joy in the work you do.

Enjoy! 😊

Sometimes, looking for a job can feel like trying to match apples with oranges. Those of us looking for work ("WORK-seekers") and those looking for workers ("WORKER-seekers") are searching to find each other. These days, we mostly rely on information technology through computers to help connect WORKER-Seekers with WORK-Seekers because this form of communication can reach more people, and offer more opportunities, than ever possible before. However, to help you find the best "fit", we shall first need to learn how to navigate in what we are calling the JOB DISCOVERY TOOLBOX.

Seeking ways to integrate our *Interests* and our *Skills* to sustain, discover or re-discover, the work we want to do and with a job we want to have.

A. Being a WORK-Seeker as a Process of Positive Discovery

Looking for work can be a process of positive DISCOVERY. When we invest ourselves as an engaged WORK-Seeker, we become more involved in discovering our own interests, skills and future possibilities. An investment-of-self is especially useful when we find ourselves in the midst of change because when change occurs, we too are changing by adding new experiences into our lives. For this reason, being informed about how the current work environment impacts us is especially important.

We can navigate through situations more meaningfully when we are aware of both our preferences and our options. Being able to comprehend and integrate our current preferences with our available options is what helps us to successfully navigate our reality, find meaning in what we do, and be more resilient when planning our futures.

As WORK-Seekers, our first activity focuses on embracing an open and positive mind-set to fully explore our existing opportunities. Sometimes, we miss recognizing our full working potential because we are not aware of how much we already understand about the many opportunities before us, unless we know how to discover these. Although the work landscape is continuously changing, this also means our work opportunities are constantly shifting as well. By fully exploring our options, we are more likely to find ways of matching our preferred interests alongside skills we can employ, and with the work we want to do.

B. Expanding Your Job Discovery Prospects

When we are working, we usually have a job title and a job description. For example, a truck driver drives a truck, or a nanny takes care of children. However, when we make a list of what we do while working, these are referred to as "job skills". Amazingly, the "skills" we have are important in many different types of work. For example, a truck driver is an expert driver, and this skill could also be useful with a postal service, a limousine company or as a driving trainer. Likewise, a nanny taking care of children can also utilize these same skills in a pre-school, the local community center offering children's activities, or even as a multi-tasking office assistant. In addition, our inventory of skills is not only developed through employment, but also evolves from community activities, volunteer accomplishments and even organizing, repairing and coordinating activity at home.

Since many different types of jobs rely on similar kinds of skills regardless of where these skills have been acquired, the way to enter the Job Discovery Toolbox is to keep in mind we will be looking for jobs across many different occupations. While a job gives a title to the work being done, an occupation describes a sector or field of knowledge and the types of experience, skills, training and education being utilized. This means similar occupations can be found across many different industries, where categories of work-places offering similar services or products are organized together. For example, an expert driving skill might be needed in the U.S. Postal Service, and this is part of the public service sector in the industry of Transportation and Warehousing. The expert skills of a nanny can transfer into a preschool setting within the industries of Education and Health Care or even into an Other-Service industry, such as a religious organization seeking an office clerk. The point is, the skills we utilize have value across different kinds of situations. Therefore, different types of occupations relying on similar skills can be found across an assortment of distinct industries.

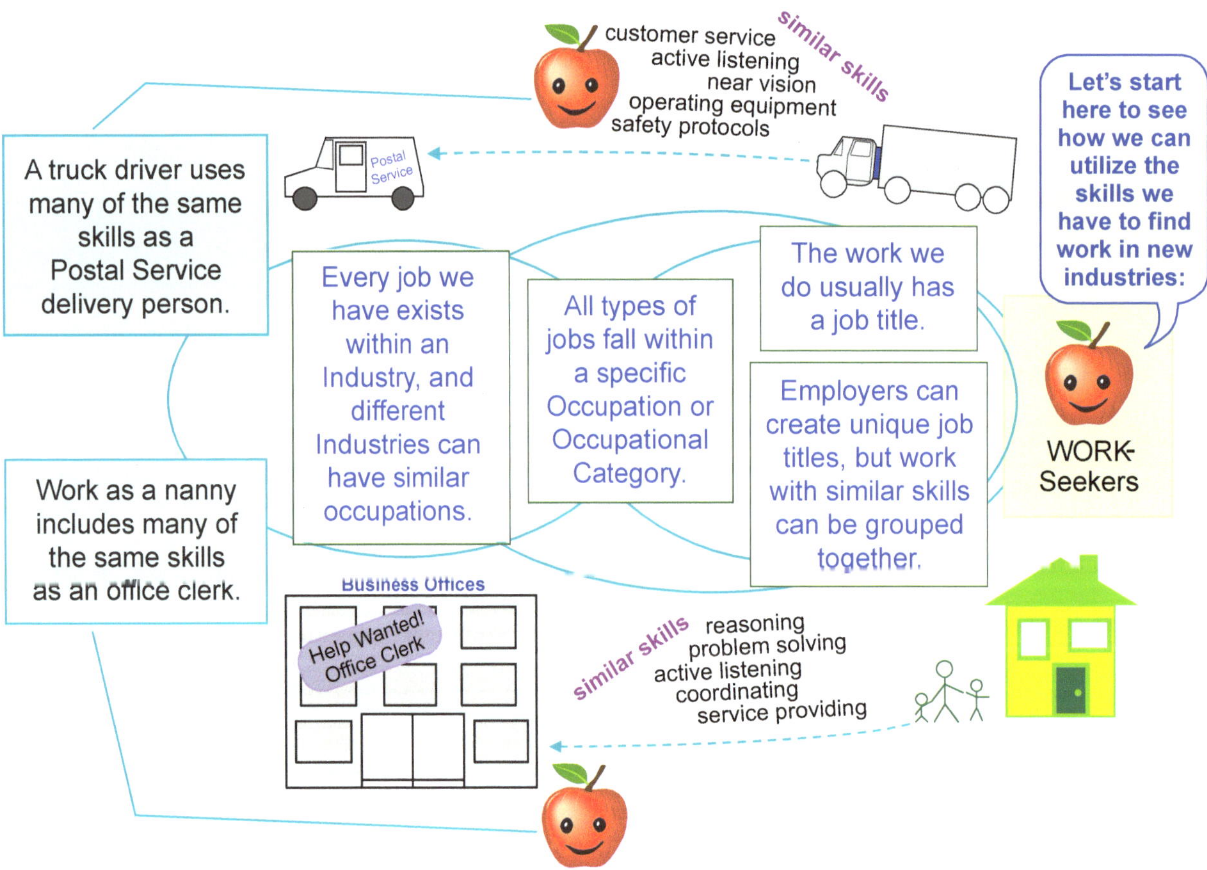

Since similar job skills are sought by employers from different industries, the way we will navigate our exploration in the Job Discovery Toolbox is to look across occupations and beyond familiar job titles.

III. UNDERSTANDING AND EXPLORING THE LABOR MARKET

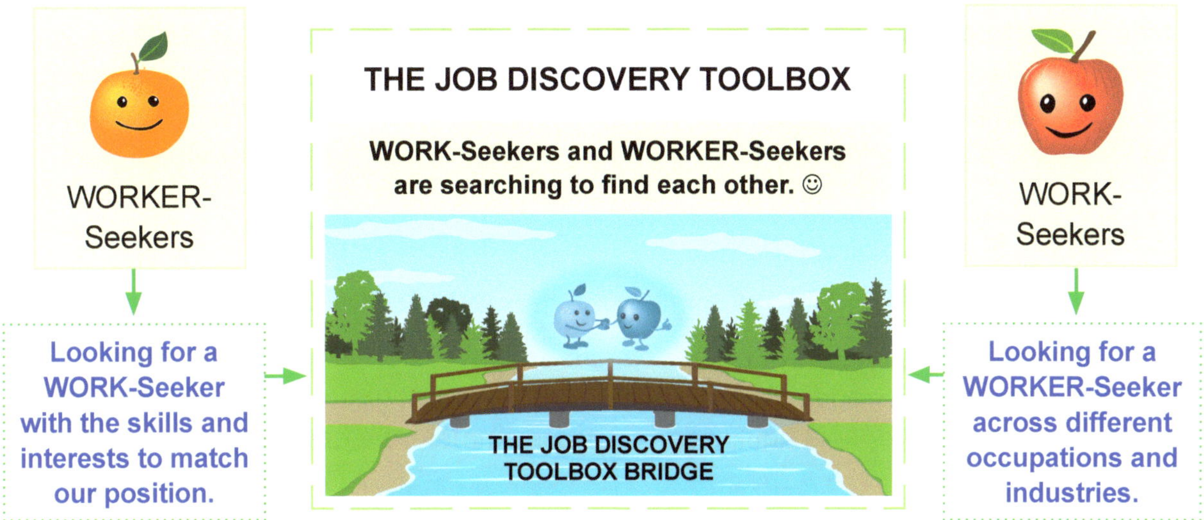

The U.S. Department of Labor (DOL) collects information across the nation on jobs, occupations and industries. This way, we can see the kinds of work people do, in what field of knowledge this work is categorized, within what types of industries, and whether the number of available jobs is growing or shrinking. For example, deforestation or cutting down trees for paper and other products used to be a high-volume activity in the Pacific Northwest. However, as we became more concerned with protecting our natural resources, this industry declined and has significantly fewer jobs today. In contrast, while deforestation was decreasing, information technology (IT) was substantially expanding. For this reason, the number of IT positions multiplied – such as being a computer technician, computer programmer or a project manager – while the number of jobs for loggers and lumberjacks fell. If you think about the number of lumberjacks you have met recently compared to the number of people working in IT, this helps illustrate how different industries grow and contract over time. However, this does not mean just because a particular occupation is in decline, a job requiring a similar set of skills cannot be found:

> A former tree-cutter was looking for a job, but no one was hiring loggers because this industry was in decline. However, given the skills possessed by this experienced tree-cutter, the forestry service was looking for a person who knew how to take care of trees so they could grow healthy and strong. Guess who qualified for this job? Yes! The former tree-cutter became a forest caretaker and was very glad to discover this new occupation.

As the example above illustrates, having a little familiarity with the Labor Market is useful because we can anticipate and understand where jobs have been, where they are now, and where they might be in the future. For example, looking for work in a declining occupation or industry means there will be fewer jobs available, unless we find ways to expand and enhance our search. **This is why the best way to look for jobs is by identifying occupations through interests and skills, instead of relying on job titles alone**. Also important is whether the occupations and industries we discover during our exploration are being phased out, remaining stable, or experiencing an exciting time of expansion.

For these reasons, Labor Market Information (LMI) is extremely useful when exploring in the Job Discovery Toolbox. Labor Market Information can reveal trends and circumstances specific to your interests. As a first example, let's walk through the Worker Adjustment and Retraining Notification (WARN) for Washington State. This is where the Employment Security Department of Washington State offers an updated list of employers giving notice about upcoming plans to close or lay-off workers, as well as other useful information.

A. An **EXAMPLE** of Utilizing Labor Market Information with WARN

1. The Worker Adjustment and Retraining Notification (WARN) Act

a. When companies in the U.S. with 100 or more employees plan to close or lay-off workers, they are required to notify their State government (usually) at least sixty days in advance. Sometimes, this notification occurs even before a company's employees are informed.

b. Although this list is always incomplete because not all employers notify the government as required, by checking this list, we can be aware in advance if a prospective employer is anticipating future layoffs or planning to close. This is useful because companies can still hire new workers even when they are planning to permanently close.

c. To find a list of companies reporting plans to lay off workers or permanently close, do an internet search for "**WARN list**" and **the State** you are interested in viewing. For example, "**WARN list**" and "**Washington State**" will provide a link to the list of WARN reporting companies at: https://esd.wa.gov/about-employees/WARN (if this website address has changed, do an internet search for "WARN List" and "Washington State" since websites can be reorganized and information moved to different webpages).

This is just one example of how Labor Market Information can provide critical signals on a larger scale, to help inform and shape our understanding of how WORK-Seekers are impacted by changing social, economic, political and environmental trends. Both WORK-Seekers and WORKER-Seekers are affected by external circumstances and as WORK-Seekers, we can become aware of situations like these to help inform our decisions.

B. What Kind of WORK-Seeker Are You at This Moment in Time?

At distinct times in our lives, we are different kinds of WORK-Seekers. For this reason, thinking about what our immediate priority is when looking for work, can help us determine how quickly a job is needed: **the more immediate the necessity, the more flexible we may need to be in order to secure a job as quickly as possible.**

Let's consider three types of possible situations we may find ourselves in as WORK-Seekers, whether we are looking for part-time or full-time work.* If we think about now as a moment in time, is finding a survival job, a gap job, or a target job the most important? When considering these three possible approaches, which one might best describe your current situation?
(*Note: Unemployment Insurance typically requires looking for full-time work.)

✓ A *survival job* means you need to be working now, and any kind of job is welcome to help pay for food and other necessities. However, while working in a Survival Job, you can still continue to prepare and look for a Target Job, perhaps with the same employer.

✓ A *gap job* describes looking for work to fill a space of time such as while waiting for a future job already guaranteed, seeking to work until graduating from school, or looking for a temporary position. Recognizing how every activity helps to continuously improve our knowledge, skills and abilities is important too, since every involvement can increase our opportunity for future work.

✓ A *target job* refers to identifying a "next step" towards your most highly desired work, perhaps within a specific career or profession. Currently, you are not in need of work, but are ready to move forward by increasing your skills to match your interests more closely. Target jobs are usually thought of as representing longer-term career interests, focused on moving towards the work you would like to do for as long as possible.

1. Discovery 1: IDENTIFYING AND ORIENTING YOUR WORK-SEEKING PRIORITIES

In this Discovery Tool, you will be asked to consider your most immediate interests in terms of exploring survival jobs, gap jobs and target jobs.

What is most relevant when thinking about your current situation as a WORK-Seeker? Are you looking for a survival job, gap job, target job, or any combination of the three?

Please place a check mark or number (1, 2, 3) to prioritize whether your most immediate objective is to look for a survival job, gap job, target job or some combination of the three.

1st Priority:	_____survival job	_____gap job	_____target job

2nd Priority:	_____survival job	_____gap job	_____target job

Again, please keep in mind if you are receiving Unemployment Insurance, this may require being available for full-time employment, even if you are willing to accept any job offer. Be sure to check with your State Unemployment office if you have any questions.

IV. AN OVERVIEW OF OUR APPROACH IN THE JOB DISCOVERY TOOLBOX

By identifying priorities based on what is most important, we can ready ourselves to step further into the Job Discovery Toolbox by focusing on where you are during this snapshot of time. The Job Discovery Toolbox will also help us to consider different Work-Seeking exploratory paths. For example, you might find a job that is almost what you want to do, but not quite. By keeping in mind and working towards your "target job", you can plan further into the future and help keep alive the passion for the kind of work you find most meaningful.

In the following sections of this Discovery-Guide, we will explore your current interests and skills, and offer ways to help creatively match these with each other. Given the accelerated unfolding rate of change still occurring in the job market following the 2020-2021+ Covid-19 pandemic and our increasing reliance on technology, this is a great time for exploring your current interests and skills. Your discoveries may cultivate a better match for perhaps, an unavoidably changing and newly emerging work landscape into the future.

In a previous section, we discussed the difference between jobs, job titles, occupations and industries. We are going to begin exploring all of these by introducing the navigational tools in our Job Discovery Toolbox to match your interests and skills with different work options.

1. We'll begin first by exploring your Interests, and then your Skills, to help you decide if there is an acceptable connection between what you are interested in and the type of work you want to look for.

2. Next, we'll identify occupational matches to help with your job search options. And if you have an interest, we'll explore different industries where you can find similar types of jobs, as well as which occupations and industries are expected to grow.

3. Along our journey, we will also investigate the tools to explore occupational categories you might find useful to consider, in terms of thinking about longer-term career opportunities.

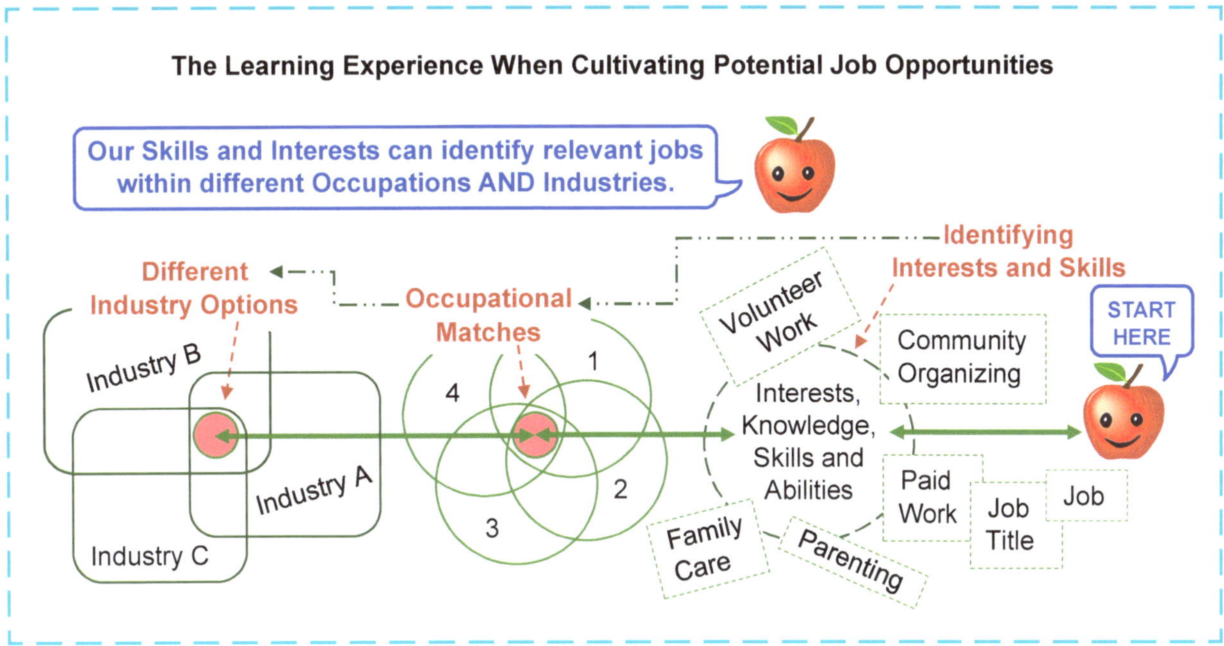

The navigational path for connecting our Interests and Skills with finding Occupational Matches within different possible Industries will occur through a series of Discovery Tools (the first one was completed earlier when prioritizing for a survival, gap, or target job). Since we will be moving towards utilizing **occupations** instead of job titles, this often includes information about longer-term **career** considerations as well. In addition, information about the different types of careers evolving from an occupation can be useful to anticipate current job stability and potential skills expansion, thereby enhancing our work opportunities into the future.

While an **occupation** (like a project management specialist) connects a type of work with a set of skills, knowledge and abilities (such as updating project plans), a **career** looks at the different kinds of expanded opportunities available across our future work-life. For example, a Project Management Specialist may eventually enjoy coordinating the activities for sets of other project management specialists. This career path would involve accumulating the additional knowledge, skills, and abilities for a slightly different occupation, such as becoming a Project Manager for a team of specialists.

When looking towards our future work-life opportunities, prospective jobs are more likely to be influenced by the creative and innovative ideas to come, rather than from past traditions. This means we can incorporate our creative ideas into our work future as well. For this reason, we will be taking a short excursion on our journey to explore a few different occupations and their corresponding careers, so you can keep these in mind as possible future extensions.

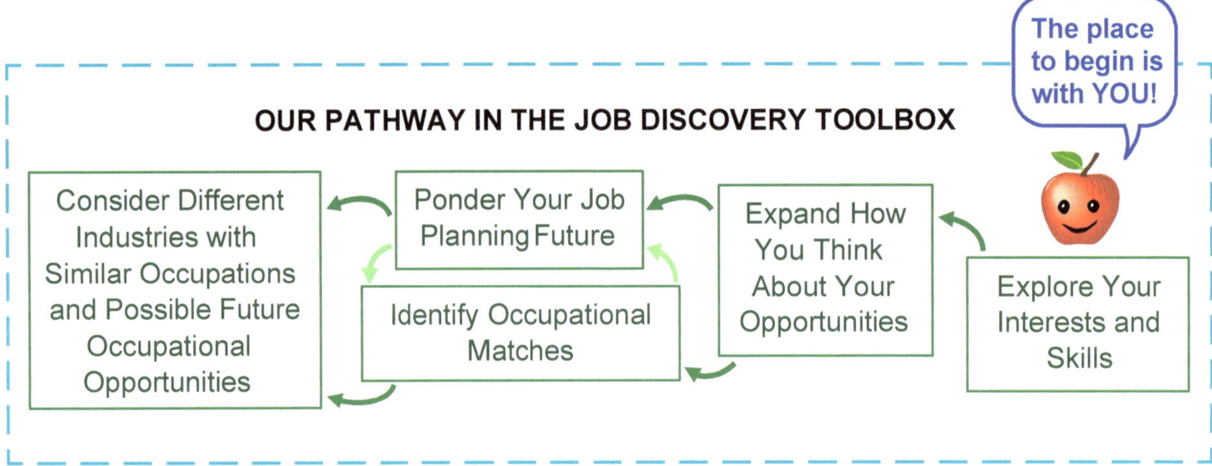

The next sections in this Discovery-Guide will navigate us through a series of Discovery Tools to:

- Expand your work opportunities by connecting your Interests and Skills with different occupational matches.

- Translate current or past work into occupational categories for expanded flexibility in job searching.

- Improve your ability to explore and consider future career plans linked with your occupational matches.

- Explore alternate industries where jobs with similar kinds of interests and skills are available.

All of the tools we will explore throughout this Discovery-Guide will support your interests, skills and decisions, not just now, but hopefully into the future as well. And, you will also have this Discovery-Guide to review and explore any new ideas you might have in the future.

Congratulations on your Great Effort so far!

(And please take a short break if this would help refresh your attention and concentration.)

When you are ready, we can move into the next section. 😊

Whether looking for a survival, gap, target job or some combination across time, considering what kind of work to look for also means thinking about both our interests and our skills. Our interests guide us towards work we enjoy and find meaningful, while our skills inform us about

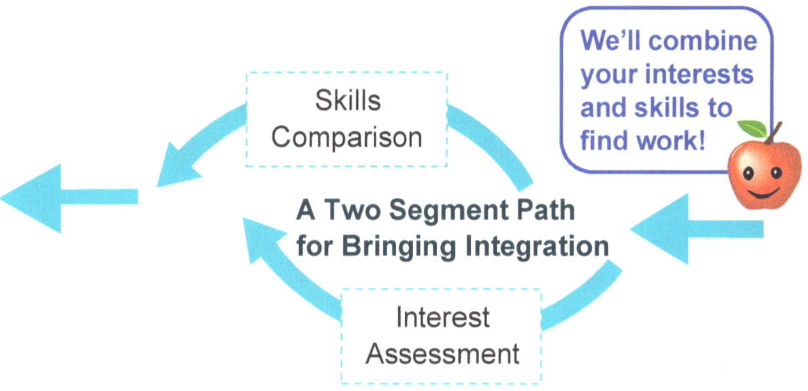

the experience and knowledge we have accumulated in our lives so far. Oftentimes, we are unaware of our accumulated skills because we just do what needs to be done, rather than write lists about what we know how to do. Likewise, we often do not truly pursue our own interests because we are focused on doing our best, at what needs to be done. By acknowledging and creating a connecting bridge between our skills and interests, we can update our understanding of where we are at this point in time, as well as spark ideas for new work aspirations into the future. Connections such as these can enliven our work-finding discoveries by revealing opportunities we did not know to explore before.

Sometimes, it's difficult to decide where to begin when starting a job search. As WORK-Seekers, we often begin by looking for work with familiar job titles. However, as explained earlier, relying only upon a job title narrows the possibility of finding relevant work.

For example, an 'office manager' was looking for other jobs with the same title. However, the job postings for 'office manager' did not actually match with her interests and skills. By exploring and discovering occupational categories instead of using the title from her previous job, she was able to identify her actual interests and skills as related to bookkeeping, data entry and budgeting – a very different set of work interests and skills than she had been searching for. And, she was able to find promising job postings too.

Places of employment create their own job titles to describe the work being done. However, as in the previous example, a job title at one place might not involve the same skills as work with the same job title at a different place. For this reason, there is the Standard Occupational Classification (SOC) defined by the U.S.

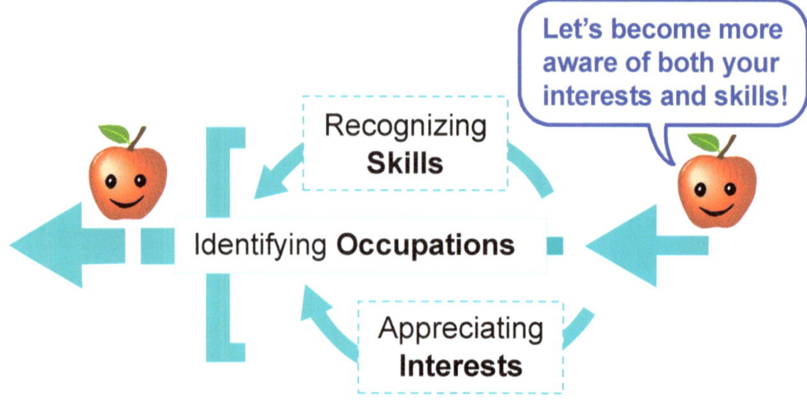

Department of Labor to help both WORK-Seekers and WORKER-Seekers find each other. When we look for work relying only on a job title, without being aware of the Standard Occupational Classification, our job search results are more limited and may not match with our experiences, interests or skill sets.

Additionally, when we work, we often engage in many different kinds of activity not accounted for by our job title. For example, if you have ever had a job where you were doing more than was outlined by your job description and job title, then looking for work with the same job title may not fully account for your current skills and interests. For these reasons, we will continue our journey of discovery in the next sections to explore an *interest* appreciation assessment and later, a *skills* appreciation comparison. Both activities will provide results identifying corresponding *occupations* to help expand our options and hopefully, allow you to validate and appreciate your interests and skills more fully.

From exploring these self-appreciation activities, you may discover interests and skills you were not aware of before, or receive affirmation about what you already know but have not fully incorporated into how you think about yourself. By comparing your interest assessment and skills comparison results, you might discover an exciting work possibility not previously considered and with resume-relevant vocabulary to use during your job search activities.

*The remainder of this Discovery-Guide will require access to a computer, as you will be working at the computer and writing in this Discovery-Guide. If you have a printed copy of the Discovery-Guide, a pen or pencil will also be needed. If you are reading this Discovery-Guide on a computer screen using two monitors – one for the Discovery-Guide where you can type information in the spaces provided, and one for exploring the websites we will be visiting – this can work too. (The pages you will be writing or typing on can be found in the Table of Contents with the blue-colored titles for **Discovery 1 - Discovery 15B**.)*

The Discovery Tools in the following sections are intended to help you explore different types of Labor Market Information, offer guidance on where various kinds of information can be found, and how to meaningfully access this. We encourage you to explore and enjoy!

VI. IDENTIFYING YOUR INTERESTS

This section will guide you through taking an Interest Assessment of 30 questions. Plan on about 10 minutes for the interest survey and another 20 minutes to review your results. Since your Interest Assessment results are not automatically stored, instructions to print, download and/or save the findings are provided by following along with the flow-chart below. After completing the Interest Assessment, the successive Discovery Tools will allow you to record your results. The information you discover will be required for exploring occupational searches at different websites in later sections of this Discovery-Guide.

After completing the Interest Assessment, a table is provided in this Discovery-Guide to record your results which will be needed when we move to a different website in the next section. Please continue to follow along with the steps provided in the flow-chart after completing your Interest Assessment, before exploring these results on your own.

Following the instructions to print or download your result descriptions can assist with additional job search and career explorations in the future.

An important note: The websites we will be visiting sometimes change the wording or website organization. If this has happened, look in these flow-chart boxes for the keywords in bolded purple, then look for the same words on the webpage (or do a search for the keyword at the website). Alternatively, updates can be found at https://www.navigatingreality.com. Look for **Learning Tools > Discovery-Guide Updates**.

1. Go to: https://www.careeronestop.org.

2. On the left side in the blue horizontal bar across the top of the webpage, select **Explore Careers**.

3. Under **Explore Careers**, look for **Self assessments**.

4. Under the title **Self assessments**, select **Interest assessment** to arrive at a new webpage.

Remember too, you can re-take this Interest Assessment as many times as you like because your preferences might change or become more refined during our exploratory journey. If the results you receive seem inaccurate, we recommend taking the Interest Assessment again.

At your computer, follow the guidance below to continue your discovery journey.

5. NOTE: After completing the Interest Assessment, you will be on a webpage where you can explore occupational careers matching your interests. **After completing the Interest Assessment and *before* exploring these results on your own, complete the next section of this Discovery-Guide to review and record your RIASEC results.**

6. On the current **Interest assessment** webpage, look towards the middle of this webpage for **Ready to take the Interest Assessment?**. (If the wording has changed, move to the next box in this flow-chart.)

7. If you see the words **Visit the Interest Assessment,** click on the words **Interest Assessment** in the first sentence. (If the wording has changed, look for the words Interest Assessment and click on this. Or, enter Interest Assessment in the search box located near the upper right corner of the webpage.)

8. Next, you will be responding to 30 questions. When completed, you will automatically be taken to a webpage with a list of occupational careers matching your Interest Assessment.

Before exploring the occupations matching your interests, complete the next page of this Discovery-Guide to review and record your RIASEC results in Discovery 2A (and 2B), which you will need for exploring occupational categories at a different website later in this Discovery-Guide.

When you are ready, select START ASSESSMENT.

Congratulations on completing the Interest Assessment - Great Work!

PLEASE NOTE: If you select "Change answers" on the upper left side of the webpage after taking the Interest Assessment, you will be able to change your responses. However, the program may not provide you with RIASEC scores after changing your responses. To receive RIASEC scores from a different set of responses, you may need to take the Interest Assessment again.

The results from your interest assessment will NOT be saved if you leave the results webpage, so let's move into the next section of this Discovery-Guide to record and explore your possibilities further. Instructions will be provided as you follow along in the flow-chart to print or save your results. 😊

When you are ready, let's move into the next section and explore your Interest Assessment suggestions. First, we will record and explore your RIASEC scores, so be sure to follow the flow-chart on the next page.

A. Exploring Your Interest Assessment

After completing the Interest Assessment, you are automatically taken to a new webpage with a list of career matches. Before exploring this list, we shall need to record your results to see if you think the career matches coincide with your interests. You know best if the results seem to describe you well, or not. Again, if your Interest Assessment results do not seem to describe you, this assessment can be taken as many times as you like, to explore different possible suggestions.

FIRST (on this Interest Assessment webpage with career matches):

<table>
<tr>
<td>

1. Before you **Explore the occupations matching your interests**, look to the left side of the webpage for a box entitled **Your Interests**.

2. In the box labeled **Your Interests** on the left side, click on **What does my score mean?** at the bottom of this box.

If you do not have any RIASEC scores, retake the Interest Assessment by returning to Step #2 in the flow-chart on page 13 of this Discovery-Guide. (Occasionally, a website error may occur.)

</td>
<td>

3. After selecting **What does my score mean?**, the next webpage will display your RIASEC Interest Assessment results. These results identify which interest categories were determined to be the strongest, based on your responses to the Interest Assessment. Write your scores in the table below on this Discovery-Guide page.

</td>
</tr>
</table>

B. DISCOVERY TOOLS 2A-2B – Reviewing Your RIASEC Results

In the table below, please write in the numbers received from your RIASEC scores in the space provided for each category. You will notice the beginning letter of each category comprises the letters RIASEC and are based on the Holland Codes. More information on the Holland Codes can be found on page 108 in the Appendix of this Discovery-Guide.

1. Discovery 2A: YOUR RIASEC SCORES

Please write in your numbered RIASEC score below for each of the categories:
Realistic (R), Investigative (I), Artistic (A), Social (S), Enterprising (E) and Conventional (C).

Realistic	Investigative	Artistic	Social	Enterprising	Conventional
R=______	I=______	A=______	S=______	E=______	C=______

Next, we shall investigate your strongest RIASEC preferences.

<table>
<tr><td>

4. Identify the interests listed under:
Based on your assessment you tested strongest below, as listed at the top of the webpage:

</td><td>

5. More information about each interest area is listed under your scores by looking to the right for the **plus (+) icons** to click on. Write your notes in the table below.

</td></tr>
</table>

2. Discovery 2B: RECORDING YOUR RIASEC INFORMATION

Record Your RIASEC information of interest in the spaces provided below.	
Record the **RIASEC areas you tested strongest in** below, as listed at the top of the webpage:	RIASEC Descriptions: In the space provided below, write a few of the relevant (or questionable) interest descriptions for each of your RIASEC codes. (Click on the **+ icon on the left side of the blue bar** for each category title to see the corresponding descriptions).
Interest Category #1: (write in a R, I, A, S, E, or C) **Letter Code:** __________	
Interest Category #2: (write in a R, I, A, S, E, or C) **Letter Code:** __________	
Interest Category #3: (write in a R, I, A, S, E, or C) **Letter Code:** __________	
Interest Category #4: (write in a R, I, A, S, E, or C) **Letter Code:** __________	

After leaving this website, you will not be able to access these results again. Follow below to **Email or Print,** or to **Save a Copy or Print.**

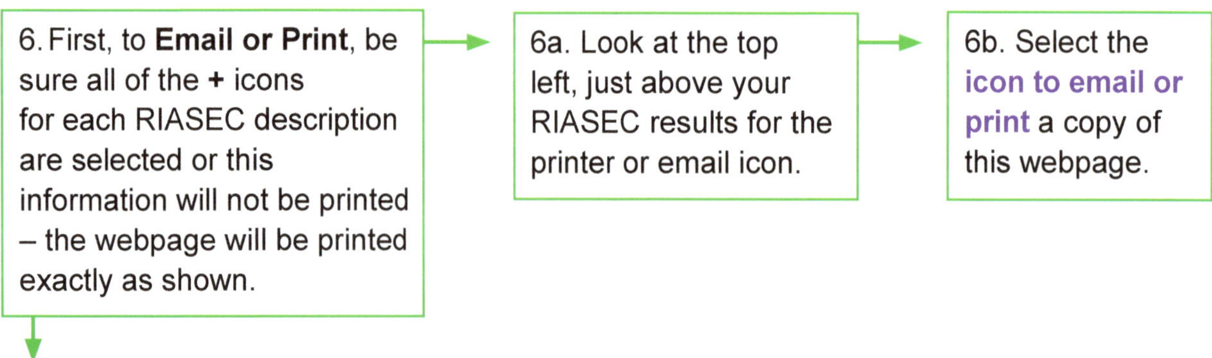

<table>
<tr><td>

6. First, to **Email or Print**, be sure all of the **+** icons for each RIASEC description are selected or this information will not be printed – the webpage will be printed exactly as shown.

</td><td>

6a. Look at the top left, just above your RIASEC results for the printer or email icon.

</td><td>

6b. Select the **icon to email or print** a copy of this webpage.

</td></tr>
</table>

OR to Download a Copy to Save and Print, go to the next page.

7. **To Download a Copy and Print** your RIASEC scores and their corresponding descriptions, look to the bottom left of the webpage (under the CONVENTIONAL category) for the word Download.

7a. Click on the word Download and select to download as a PDF, Word or RTF document file. You can then save the file on your computer or a USB flash drive. You may want to rename the document file and decide where you would like to save this, for further review at a later time.

7b. If you would also like to **Print a Copy** of your results, open the file you just saved and print a copy. Alternatively, on the webpage, make sure you have opened all the green down arrows for each RIASEC category description, since whatever you see on the webpage is what will be printed. Look above your RIASEC scores (near the top of the webpage) for the printer icon and click on this to print.

8. To return to the previous webpage and continue in this Discovery-Guide, look under the **Interest Assessment** heading on the top left of the webpage, just to the left of the print and email icons.

Under the **Interest Assessment** heading, select Back to results.

9. When you are on the webpage with the words **We found __careers matching your interest assessment** near the top of the webpage (under the printer icon), go to the next page in this Discovery-Guide and complete the Discovery Tools 3A, 3B and 3C to record information about your potential occupational career matches.

MOVE TO THE NEXT PAGE AND RECORD YOUR POSSIBLE OCCUPATIONAL CAREER MATCHES

C. DISCOVERY TOOLS 3A-3C – Recording Your Initial Interest Matches

Although most of our occupational searches will occur at a different website, you can begin to explore and record information about the occupational careers you find most interesting.

1. Discovery 3A: YOUR OCCUPATIONAL INTEREST CAREER MATCHES

First, record information for any of the occupational careers matching your interests below by entering the occupations you find most interesting in the table below. This will be useful when we explore your options at a different website later in this Discovery-Guide. Additional occupational matches can be found by looking to see if more webpages are listed at the bottom right of the webpage. **Click on any title listed under Career** for more detailed information about Wages, Future Demand, etc. You can record more in-depth information for TWO matches on the next pages of this Discovery-Guide.

Strength of **Match**	**Career** Match Title or Description	Future Demand **Outlook**	**Hourly Wages**	Typical **Education**
1.				
2.				
3.				
4.				
5.				

10. Select the FIRST OF TWO occupational interest matches to explore, by clicking on an occupational title under **Career**. Write any notes in the table below.

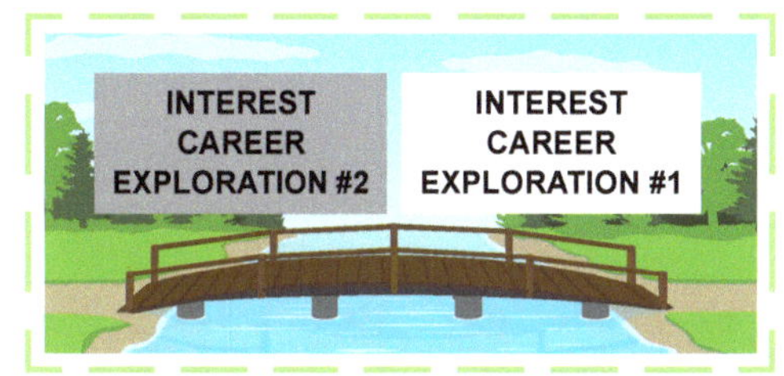

2. *Discovery 3B: EXPLORING INTEREST CAREER #1*

Write in a Title to Explore:	Space is provided for you to write in Self-Notes below.
Description: what do they do? Alternative titles under "Also known as:"	
Career Video: Some of the profiles include a short video about this career.	
Outlook: will there be jobs? Indicates the future outlook for this career. ***Find current job openings by selecting Find job openings** at the bottom left corner.	
Projected Employment *Select **Compare Projected Employment** to see the predicted job outlook by city, state, or ZIP code.	
Typical Wages ***Most wages are usually between 10-25%.**	
Education and Experience: to get started Common educational requirements and experience for this career.	
Typical education *Where most workers in this career are. *Provides a list of activities most people in this career do during a typical day.	
Certifications: show your skills *To enhance skills and resumes.	
Licenses: do you need one? *Find licensing information by state.	
Apprenticeships: learn on the job *Not common; internships might be possible.	
Activities: what you might do in a day *Select **More activities** for additional info.	
Knowledge ***These descriptions can help with a resume.**	
Skills ***These descriptions can help with a resume.**	
Abilities ***These descriptions can help with a resume.**	
Related Occupations ***Select More occupations for an extended list of related occupations.**	

<table>
<tr><td>11. Return to the previous webpage by using the browser's back arrow. Choose a SECOND occupational career match to explore further by clicking on the title. Write any information of interest in the table below.</td><td>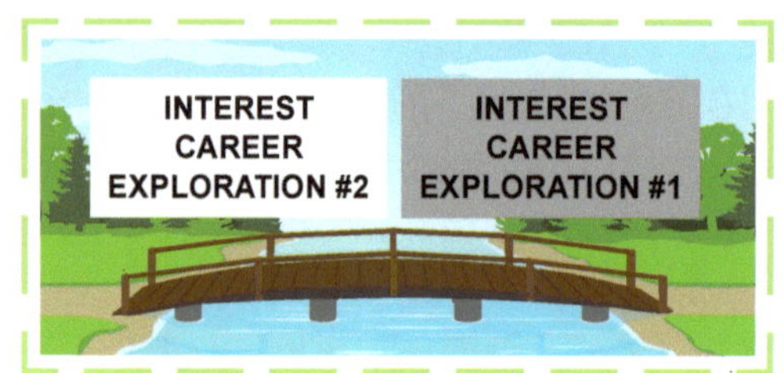</td></tr>
</table>

3. *Discovery 3C: EXPLORING INTEREST CAREER #2*

Write in a Title to Explore:	Space is provided for you to write in Self-Notes below.
Description: what do they do? Alternative titles under "Also known as:"	
Career Video: Some of the profiles include a short video about this career.	
Outlook: will there be jobs? Indicates the future outlook for this career. ***Find current job openings by selecting** **Find job openings** at the bottom left corner.	
Projected Employment *Select **Compare Projected Employment** to see the predicted job outlook by city, state, or ZIP code.	
Typical Wages ***Most wages are usually between 10-25%.**	
Education and Experience: to get started Common educational requirements and experience for this career.	
Typical education *Where most workers in this career are. *Provides a list of activities most people in this career do during a typical day.	
Certifications: show your skills *To enhance skills and resumes.	
Licenses: do you need one? *Find licensing information by state.	
Apprenticeships: learn on the job *Not common; internships might be possible.	
Activities: what you might do in a day *Select **More activities** for additional info.	
Knowledge ***These descriptions can help with a resume.**	
Skills ***These descriptions can help with a resume.**	
Abilities ***These descriptions can help with a resume.**	
Related Occupations ***Select More occupations for an extended list of related occupations.**	

CONGRATULATIONS and GREAT WORK!

D. A Discovery Roadmap Refresher

You have completed an exploration of your interests and next, we will identify and explore an appreciation of your skills to determine how closely you think your interests and skills are connected with the work you have done, would like to do more of, or would like to develop a future plan for. After completing a Skills Comparison activity, we will work on connecting your occupational selections based on both your Interest Assessment and Skills Comparison results by first, moving between two different websites (and later, adding two additional ones).

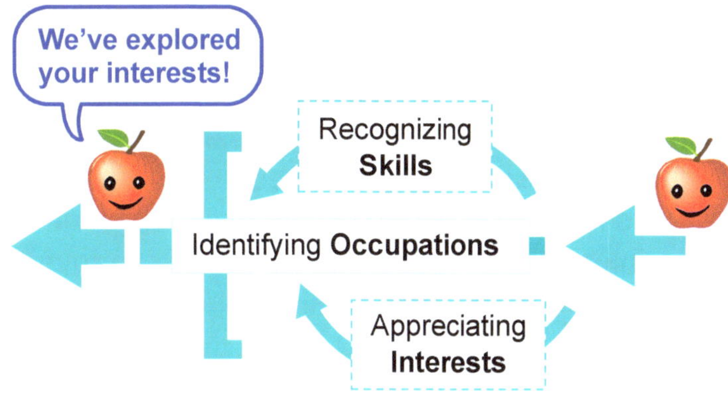

The website we are currently at is https://www.careeronestop.org/, which relies on occupational categories to identify possible career pathways. This means for every occupation identified in your Interest Assessment results, there is a potential pathway for continued learning through a possible career trajectory in this type of work. However, with our rapidly changing post-pandemic work environment impacting the types of jobs available and how places of work shall operate in the future, many of us will find ourselves utilizing our interests and skills to cultivate our own unique career paths. Just as the logger mentioned in an earlier example became a forest caretaker, the constant changing landscape of jobs can also mean there are more creative pathways for employing your interests and skills together.

We will be working across two different websites:

careeronestop   🌐 Español

Your source for career exploration, training & jobs

Sponsored by the U.S. Department of Labor. A proud partner of the americanjobcenter network.

O*NET OnLine

O*NET OnLine is sponsored by the U.S. Department of Labor, Employment & Training Administration, and developed by the National Center for O*NET Development.

Organizing Occupational Categories to Outline Career Descriptions and Pathways

Organizing Occupational Categories to Describe Knowledge, Skills and Abilities.

To help us find a job now and think about our future.

Since we shall experience ongoing change in our working environments through innovative technologies as well socio-economic developments, we will initially explore two different websites – one looking at occupations as careers and career pathways (where we currently are in this Discovery-Guide at careeronestop.org), and a different website (onetonline.org) offering more comprehensive information about specific occupations to support job searches and resume writing. This second website will identify and describe your knowledge, skills and abilities (KSAs) based on industry standards with terminology most employers understand (because employers contribute to this information collected by the US. Department of Labor). Both websites help us to see the work we do from slightly different perspectives so we can successfully find the words to:

1. describe what we have done in the past,

2. explain what we are working on now, and

3. convey the kind of work we have an interest in doing or working towards in the future.

As we move across and between different websites, we will begin to expand our Job Discovery Toolbox Tools to explore occupations and possible future interests more creatively. This Discovery-Guide will continue to have Discovery Tools for recording the information you are gathering, so the tools and skills you are accumulating can be utilized into the future.

If you would like to refresh yourself and take a short break, now would be a time to do this, before moving into exploring your skills through a Skills Appreciation review. 😊

 COMPARING YOUR SKILLS ACROSS DIFFERENT OCCUPATIONAL CAREER OPTIONS

Instead of doing an assessment on Skills, we are going to explore the skills you have in relation to your past experiences. This way, you can see how closely your past endeavors are connected with the results from your Interest Assessment. To begin, follow along with the flow-chart below. Again, there will be Discovery Tools provided in this Discovery-Guide for recording information about your occupational results to assist with your job search efforts.

1. Go to https://www.careeronestop.org. If you are already at this website, continue to the next step. (Don't see what you're looking for on a webpage? Look in the flow-charts for the bolded purple terms and do a search or go to https://www.navigatingreality.com/discovery-guide-updates to download pages with updated instructions. If you've found changes before us, please let us know!)

2. Select **Explore Careers** at the top left of the webpage, in the blue horizontal bar.

3. Under the title **Self assessments**, select **Skills Assessment** to arrive at a new webpage.

4. **NOTE: Again, after completing the Skills Comparison, a table is provided in this Discovery-Guide to record your results. Continue following along with the flow-charts to keep track of the information you are collecting about possible occupational career matches.**

5. On the Skills Assessment webpage is information to consider about different categories of skills and what employers look for. There is a detailed Skills Matcher assessment on this webpage too. However, we are going to a different website for a more flexible approach, and to expand your set of tools.

6a. For next website (we will return to careeronestop shortly) go to https://www.myskillsmyfuture.org and continue following the flow-chart.

6b. If you want to click on **Take the Skills Matcher** in the middle of this webpage, you can do so (or move to 6a now). On the next webpage, click on **START SKILLS MATCHER**. When finished with the Skills Matcher, return here and resume your activity with 6a, to the left of this box.

7. At myskillsmyfuture.org, look for the blue colored box with the title **Build a bridge to your new career**. Inside this blue box will be a place to Enter your current or past job.

8. In the space provided, enter a current or past job title, occupation, or even the title of volunteer work where you have acquired skills. Then select **FIND MY CAREER MATCHES.**

9. **If you have received career matches** closely related to your past or current work, proceed to step #10 on the next page of this Discovery-Guide.

9a. **If you do not receive career matches** relevant to current or past work, we probably need to translate the job title you used into an occupational category first, by moving to the next flow-chart box, just to the right of this one.

GO HERE IF YOU DO NOT RECEIVE CAREER MATCHES.

9b. If you can, open a new browser window and go to https://www.onetonline.org.

9c. At the very top right side of this webpage are the words **Occupation keyword search**.

9d. Under **Occupation keyword search**, **type in a current or past job title** (do not use the drop-down menu) and tap **Enter** on your keyboard (**Return** on a Mac) or click on the word **Go**, to the right of your entry.

9e. On your **Occupation Keyword Search** results webpage, write in one or two of the occupations listed in the space provided below.

(1) __________________________

____

(2) __________________________

____

9f. We will spend more time exploring onetonline.org in the next Discovery-Guide section. For now, return to https://www.myskillsmyfuture.org to resume your Skills Comparison.

9g. On the https://www.myskillsmyfuture.org/ homepage, look for the blue colored box with the title **Build a bridge to your new career**. Inside this blue box will be a place to **Enter your current or past job**.

9h. Enter a past, current job or occupation from the two just identified above during your "Occupation keyword search" at onetonline.org (9d. above) and click on **FIND MY CAREER MATCHES.** This will take you to a new webpage.

10. Under the words **The careers below may be a good match for** is a box with an arrow next to the occupation you entered. **Click on the arrow** for a list of similar career categories. **If relevant, select your closest match from the list.**

11. Under the heading **Occupation** on the left side of the webpage, you can compare your skills with a possible match by selecting **Compare Skills**. This option is listed under each occupational title and will compare skill sets within the occupational career category you selected at the top of this webpage. We will focus more on comparing occupations in a later section of this Discovery-Guide.

A. DISCOVERY TOOLS 4A-4C – Identifying Similar Careers of Interest Based on Your Skills

In the table below and after comparing the skills from similar career matches based on the jobs you entered to **Find My Career Matches** (including any jobs from volunteer work you have entered), write in four or five Career Matches from the list under the **Occupation** column most relevant to your skills and/or interests. Or, record your relevant information below, if you opted for the Skills Matcher assessment instead.

1. *Discovery 4A: POSSIBLE OCCUPATIONAL SKILLS CAREER MATCHES*

List any of the titles under the **Occupation** column you would like to explore further, from the Skills Career Matches listed on this webpage.	Below is space for you to write Self-Notes and include reminders such as Salary, Similar Skills, Skill and Knowledge Gaps, Education or Training Required, etc.
1.	
2.	
3.	
4.	
5.	

12. With your list of possible occupational career matches from the previous Discovery-Guide page, we will return to careeronestop.org to complete two occupational explorations, similar to the ones you did with your Interest Assessment matches.

13. Go to https://www.careeronestop.org and click on **Explore Careers** near the top left of the webpage. This will take you to a new webpage entitled **Explore careers** with the question: **What kind of career will fit you best?** (to the left-of-center near the top of the webpage).

14. Look for the blue-grey box on the far-right side with the title **Occupational Profile**, where there is an option to **Search by Occupation**. **In the space provided, enter in one of your Possible Occupational Skills Career Matches** identified on the previous page of this Discovery-Guide. (You can record any useful information in the tables on the next pages).

15. In the box entitled **Location**, entering in a city, state, or ZIP code will provide more geographically specific information about an occupational career. If you prefer general, rather than location-specific information, enter US or United States.

16. Then, click on **Search**. On the next pages of this Discovery-Guide are tables to record information for TWO of your searches.

Information from TWO of your search results can be recorded on the next two pages.

17. If you receive a list of possible occupations, select the FIRST OF TWO occupational skills career matches to explore. Write any notes of interest in the table below.

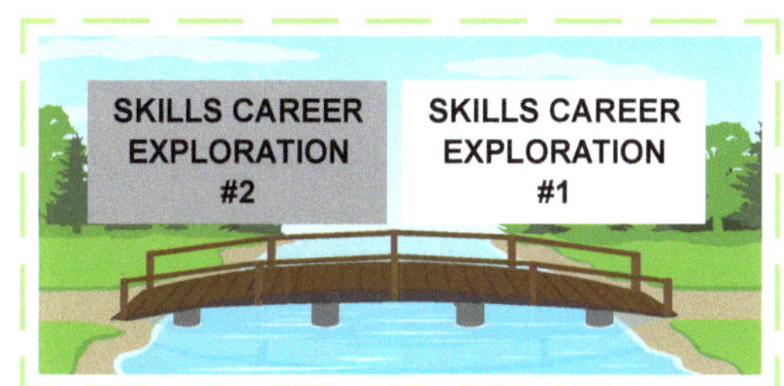

2. Discovery 4B: EXPLORING SKILLS CAREER #1

Write in the Occupational Title you are exploring:	Space is provided for you to write in Self-Notes below.
Description: what do they do? Alternative titles under "Also known as:"	
Career Video: Some of the profiles include a short video about this career.	
Outlook: will there be jobs? Indicates the future outlook for this career. ***Find current job openings by selecting Find job openings** at the bottom left corner.	
Projected Employment *Select **Compare Projected Employment** to see the predicted job outlook by city, state, or ZIP code.	
Typical Wages ***Most wages are usually between 10-25%.**	
Education and Experience: to get started Common educational requirements and experience for this career.	
Typical education *Where most workers in this career are. *Provides a list of activities most people in this career do during a typical day.	
Certifications: show your skills *To enhance skills and resumes.	
Licenses: do you need one? *Find licensing information by state.	
Apprenticeships: learn on the job *Not common; internships might be possible.	
Activities: what you might do in a day *Select **More activities** for additional info.	
Knowledge ***These descriptions can help with a resume.**	
Skills ***These descriptions can help with a resume.**	
Abilities ***These descriptions can help with a resume.**	
Related Occupations ***Select More occupations for an extended list of related occupations.**	

18. To explore a new Skills Career, click on **Explore Careers** near the top left. Enter another **Occupation** (p. 25), preferred **Location** and click on **Search** again. Then, if a list appears, select a SECOND match.

3. *Discovery 4C: EXPLORING SKILLS CAREER #2*

Write in the Occupational Title you are exploring:	Space is provided for you to write in Self-Notes below.
Description: what do they do? Alternative titles under "Also known as:"	
Career Video: Some of the profiles include a short video about this career.	
Outlook: will there be jobs? Indicates the future outlook for this career. ***Find current job openings by selecting Find job openings** at the bottom left corner.	
Projected Employment *Select **Compare Projected Employment** to see the predicted job outlook by city, state, or ZIP code.	
Typical Wages ***Most wages are usually between 10-25%.**	
Education and Experience: to get started Common educational requirements and experience for this career.	
Typical education *Where most workers in this career are. *Provides a list of activities most people in this career do during a typical day.	
Certifications: show your skills *To enhance skills and resumes.	
Licenses: do you need one? *Find licensing information by state.	
Apprenticeships: learn on the job *Not common; internships might be possible.	
Activities: what you might do in a day *Select **More activities** for additional info.	
Knowledge ***These descriptions can help with a resume.**	
Skills ***These descriptions can help with a resume.**	
Abilities ***These descriptions can help with a resume.**	
Related Occupations ***Select More occupations for an extended list of related occupations.**	

Excellent! You have completed both the Interest Appreciation Assessment and Skills Appreciation Comparison portions of this Discovery-Guide. 😊 Next, we will be moving from careeronestop.org to onetonline.org (or if you did not receive relevant career matches earlier, we will be returning to onetonline.org) for a more in-depth look at occupations and job search matches.

Before we move into the next part of this Discovery-Guide, let's take a moment to reflect on and consolidate the information you have gathered so far for easier access, since this information will be needed to further expand your job search options.

VIII. CONSOLIDATING OUR INFORMATION FROM THE PREVIOUS SECTIONS

A. DISCOVERY TOOLS 5A-5D – Consolidating Your Interests, Skills, and Potential Career Opportunity Information

First, you will need to use your RIASEC results at the next website because some of your occupation and possible job searches can be based on your interests.

1. *Discovery 5A: YOUR RIASEC SCORES*

First, let's re-enter the LETTER CODES (first letters R, I, A, S, E, C,) you received for your highest RIASEC results from the Interest Assessment. You may have 2, 3, or 4 highest scores and these were recorded on pages 15-16 in this Discovery-Guide.

Below, re-enter your highest R, I, A, S, E, or C results from the Interest Assessment (recorded on page 16): Example: (1) _____R_____

(1) _________   (2) _________   (3) _________   (4) _________

Next, let's reconsider the **Interest Career Matches** you explored earlier and identify two or three you would like to take a more in-depth look at.

2. *Discovery 5B: YOUR INTEREST ASSESSMENT MATCHES*

Enter the **Interest** Career Matches you explored earlier and would like to investigate further, which we will do in the next section of this Discovery-Guide. The Interest Matches you listed are on page 18, (and pages 19-20) in this Discovery-Guide.

Enter **Two (or more) INTEREST Career Matches** to explore when we move to the next website:

    a. Interest Career Match #1: _______________________________________

    b. Interest Career Match #2: _______________________________________

    c. List any other Interest Career Matches you would like to consider:

    ____

Let's also refine your **Skills Comparison Career Matches** to identify any of these you would like to take a more in-depth look at.

3. *Discovery 5C: YOUR SKILLS COMPARISON MATCHES*

Based on the results from your **Skills Comparison**, enter the Career Matches you explored earlier, or are interested in exploring further, when we move into the next section of this Discovery-Guide. The Skills Appreciation Career Matches you listed are on page 25 (and pages 27-28) of this Discovery-Guide.

Enter **Two (or more) SKILLS Career Matches** to explore at the next website we will move to:

    a. Skills Career Match #1: ____

    b. Skills Career Match #2: ____

    c. List any other Skills Career Matches you would like to consider:

    ____

    ____

Additionally, let's attempt to connect your Interest Career Matches with your Skills Comparison Career Matches because later in this Discovery-Guide, we will be comparing these occupations with each other.

4. *Discovery 5D: YOUR INTEREST ASSESSMENT AND SKILLS COMPARISON MATCHES*

When comparing your Interest Matches with your Skills Comparison Matches in the two previous **Discovery Tools 5B and 5C**, are there any similarities or commonalities highlighting a connection or shared theme between your interests and skills?

List any **overlapping or similar Occupational Career Matches from both your Interests and Skills** to explore at the next website.

    a. Similar Career Match #1: ____

    b. Similar Career Match #2: ____

    c. Are there any other intersecting Interest and Skills Careers you would like to explore further?

       ____

       ____

We will now move into a more in-depth exploration of occupational categories for matching your Interests and your Skills with possible jobs and their corresponding resume-relevant terminology.

Ready for a break to stretch and re-focus? Now would be a good time. ☺

IX. TRANSLATING INTERESTS AND SKILLS CAREER MATCHES INTO OCCUPATIONS

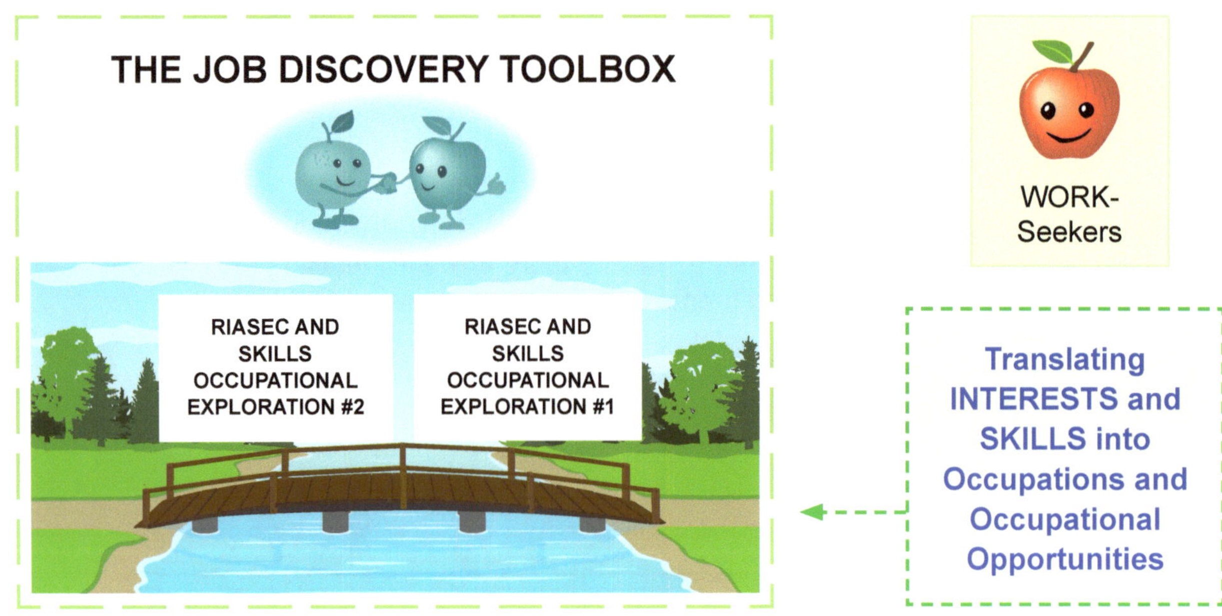

Next, we will focus on occupational searches by initially translating your RIASEC Interest results into occupational categories. We will do the same for your Skills Comparison Career Matches. Then, we will spend a little time comparing occupations so you can explore how best to connect your interests and skills with occupational options into the future.

X. EXPLORING YOUR RIASEC OCCUPATIONS

As a reminder, the website we have primarily been working from up until now has been careeronestop.org, which matches possible careers with results from different Interest and Skills identification activities. We are now going to move (or return, if you were here earlier) to onetonline.org. As mentioned earlier, onetonline.org is specifically designed to identify occupations and occupational categories thereby expanding our job searches beyond job titles.

Follow along with the flow-chart below to enter *O*net OnLine* for an inventory of different occupations. First, we will work with your RIASEC **Interest** results and later, your **Skills** Career matches. Remember to record information about your occupational searches in this Discovery-Guide. During each of the occupational Discovery Tool explorations at onetonline.org, you will also be able to have a first glance of current job openings for your consideration by clicking on the option **Job Openings on the Web** (this is also in bold letters within the Discovery Tool tables where you will record information in this Discovery-Guide). We will introduce a more expansive job search strategy at the end of this Discovery-Guide.

Important note: Remember these websites might be periodically updated. If the flow-chart instructions are different than what's on the webpage, look for the **bolded purple color** terms in the flow-charts (below) and find those terms on the webpage to click on, or do a search for the term in the upper right corner search box. We try to keep a list of the updates at https://www.navigatingreality.com/discovery-guide-updates. You can download pages with updated instructions or please let us know if you find changes before we do, by sending us an email with the page number through the contact form on our website. Thank you!

---

1. On your computer, go to https://www.onetonline.org.

2. At the top left of the webpage, look for the heading **O*NET OnLine**. Directly under this, look for the words **O*NET Data**.

3. Click on the heading **O*net Data**, then select **Interests**. This will take you to a new webpage.

4. On this next webpage labeled **Browse by Interests** will be a list of RIASEC descriptions. Select ONE of your strongest RIASEC results from your Interest Assessment taken earlier (your results are listed on page 29 or pages 15-16). **Select Realistic, Investigative, Artistic, Social, Enterprising or Conventional** and this will take you to a new webpage.

5. On this next webpage, also entitled **Browse by Interests**, look for the **boxes inside the light blue bar across the webpage**. In the box on the left side, your first interest will already be listed. **Select your next strongest RIASEC result by** clicking on the **arrow inside the box** for your **Second interest, and then your Third** (if applicable).
You will be able to record your information on the next page in this Discovery-Guide.

6. Select **GO** and a list of Occupations matching your RIASEC results will appear below the blue rectangle box. Below the blue box will be the list of your RIASEC result(s) in bold type and below this, you will see your occupational matches by: **Interest Code – Job Zone – Code – Occupation**.

- Under **Interests Code**, the order of your RIASEC categories can influence the occupations listed. **You can alter the order of your RIASEC results to see how the recommendations change by clicking on the down arrow for each RIASEC category you identified**.

- Under **Job Zone**, the numbers 1, 2, 3, 4 or 5 will provide information on the amount of preparation needed for each occupation listed.

- The **Code** is a designated occupational code as referenced in the Dictionary of Occupational Titles (DOT) with over 13,000 types of work and published by the U.S. Department of Labor. For more information about the DOT, see Appendix B Glossary of Terms or go to https://www.dol.gov/agencies/oalj/topics/libraries/LIBDOT.

- On the right side, under **Occupation**, is an inventory of different occupations matching your RIASEC results.

7. You are currently at a webpage with a list of occupations matching your RIASEC results. **On the next page of this Discovery-Guide is a table for you to record all of your occupations of interest**.

8. Before selecting one of the occupations listed, move to the next page of this Discovery-Guide to record those occupations you would like to explore more fully.

Complete Discovery 6A – 6C on the following pages of this Discovery-Guide.

Move to the next page and record your informational results.

A. DISCOVERY TOOLS 6A-6C – Selecting Two RIASEC Occupations to Explore

In the table below, identify and write in at least TWO occupations of interest from the list matching your RIASEC results (on the webpage **Browse by Interests** from steps #7-8 in the flow-chart on the previous page of this Discovery-Guide). You may also want to consider possible occupational careers listed from your careeronestop.org RIASEC results identified on pages 25, 27 or 28 in this Discovery-Guide.

1. *Discovery 6A: IDENTIFYING TWO RIASEC INTERESTS TO EXPLORE FURTHER*

Write in TWO (or more) different occupations to explore further.	
a. RIASEC OCCUPATION #1	b. RIASEC OCCUPATION #2
c. Below, list any additional RIASEC Occupations you would like to identify for additional exploration.	

Next, you will be able to consider TWO occupations of your choosing from those identified above to investigate in more detail and depth.

In the table on the next page of this Discovery-Guide, after selecting an occupation to explore further, some of the items are listed in bold letters to highlight information found to be useful:

- Under the occupational title at the top of the webpage is a **Sample of Reported Job Titles** listing other job titles employers used for this occupation.
- The **Knowledge, Skills and Abilities** (or KSAs) can help with resume building as this provides a universal language relevant for each occupation.
- **The Wage and Employment Trends** provide information about local average wages and whether this occupation is expected to increase or decrease in the number of jobs.
- The **Job Openings on the Web** identifies current employment opportunities by selecting a ZIP code, state and the website you would like to search (the most commonly used is Indeed).

9. On your computer screen, **select your FIRST OF TWO** occupations you identified on the previous Discovery-Guide page. This will take you to another screen. Here, you will find information relevant to this occupation. Record any useful information in the table below.

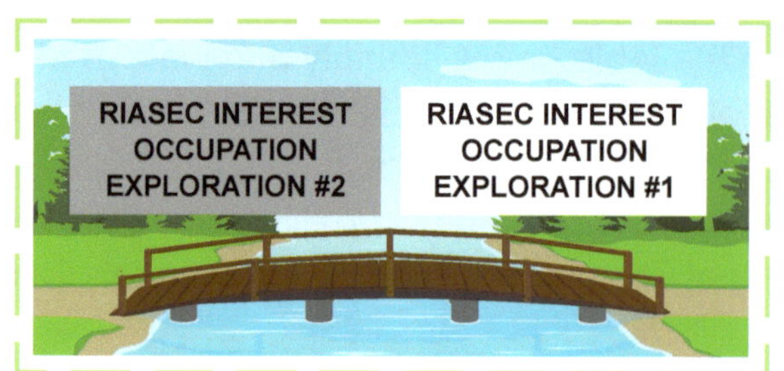

Title of Interest Occupation #1: _______________________________	Feel free to write in any information or notes to yourself below:
• **Sample of Reported Job Titles** • Tasks • Technology Skills • Work Activities • Detailed Work Activities • Work Context • Job Zone • Training & Credentials • Apprenticeship Opportunities • **Skills** • **Knowledge** • Education • **Abilities** • Interests • Work Values • Work Styles • **Wage and Employment Trends** • **Job Openings on the Web** • Related Occupations Additional Information	

10. On your computer, return to the previous screen with your RIASEC occupational results by **clicking on the browser's back arrow. Select a SECOND occupation** to explore (from your list on page 35). Below, you can explore this occupation further.

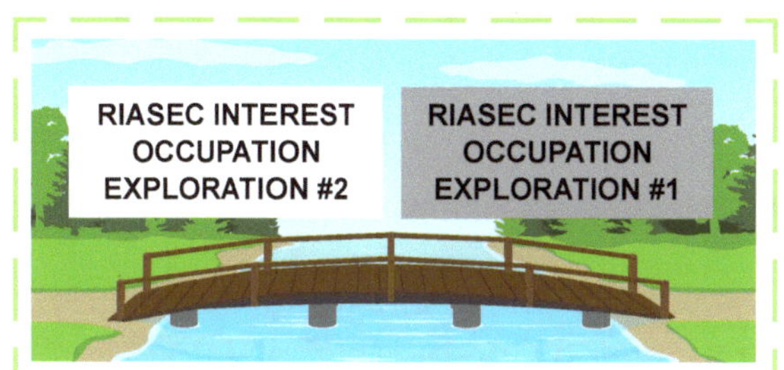

Title of Interest Occupation #2: ___________________________	Feel free to write in any information or notes to yourself below:
• **Sample of Reported Job Titles** • Tasks • Technology Skills • Work Activities • Detailed Work Activities • Work Context • Job Zone • Training & Credentials • Apprenticeship Opportunities • **Skills** • **Knowledge** • Education • **Abilities** • Interests • Work Values • Work Styles • **Wage and Employment Trends** • **Job Openings on the Web** • Related Occupations Additional Information	

CONGRATULATIONS! You have completed the RIASEC INTEREST occupations exploration portion of this Job Discovery Toolbox Discovery-Guide. 😊

XI. EXPLORING YOUR SKILLS COMPARISON OCCUPATIONS OF INTEREST

We will now move into translating your Skills Comparison Career Matches into Occupations and Occupational categories.

1. From **page 30 for Discovery Tool 5C** on **Your Skills Comparison Matches**, choose at least **TWO** matches to explore further. In the table provided below, write the **Two Skills Matches** you are interested in comparing.

Translating Your SKILLS CAREER MATCHES into Occupations and Occupational Options

A. DISCOVERY TOOLS 7A-7D – Selecting Two Skills Career Match Occupations To Explore Further

1. Discovery 7A: IDENTIFYING TWO SKILLS MATCH CAREER OCCUPATIONS

Write in TWO Skills Comparison Matches (from pages 30 or 25 of this Discovery-Guide).	
a. SKILLS CAREER MATCH #1	b. SKILLS CAREER MATCH #2

2. Again, tables are provided on the next pages of this Discovery-Guide for you to record information from TWO Skills Comparison Occupational searches.

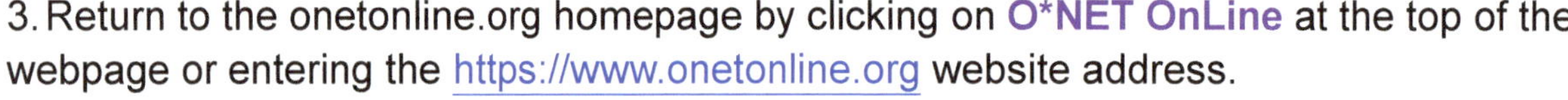

3. Return to the onetonline.org homepage by clicking on **O*NET OnLine** at the top of the webpage or entering the https://www.onetonline.org website address.

Next, you will be utilizing this Job Discovery Toolbox Discovery-Guide to consider each occupation identified above in more depth and detail.

4. On the O*Net Online homepage, look for the **Occupation keyword search** on the left side of the webpage under **O*NET OnLine features** and **Introduction**. Under **Occupation Keyword Search** is a box to type in.

Previously on page 24 of this Discovery-Guide, you may have become familiar with the "Occupation keyword search" option. This is a great option for translating job titles into occupations.

5. In the space provided below the words **Occupation Keyword Search**, type in ONE of the Skills Career Matches you identified in the table on the previous page – Discovery Tool 7A. **Do not select from the drop-down menu**. Then, click below on Search O*NET-SOC occupations.

6. The next webpage entitled **Occupation Keyword Search** will have a list of **Occupations matching** your entry. (If you do not see a list of occupations, re-enter the occupation again, but do not select from the categories in the drop-down menu.)

For a more comprehensive list, click on Show matches: All (instead of Closest) above the list of occupations. **First, complete the table below to identify your occupations of interest from this webpage. Then, proceed to the next two pages of this Discovery-Guide to record information for TWO different Skills Match Occupations.**

2. Discovery 7B: SKILLS MATCH OCCUPATIONS OF INTEREST

List any relevant **occupations of interest** from your Skills Comparison:

a. SKILLS MATCH OCCUPATION #1	b. SKILLS MATCH OCCUPATION #2

c. Other Skills Match Occupations you are interested in exploring:

Again, in the tables on the next pages of this Discovery-Guide, some of the items are listed in bold letters to highlight information most often found to be useful:

- Under the occupational title at the top of the webpage is a **Sample of Reported Job Titles** listing other job titles employers used for this occupation.

- The **Knowledge, Skills and Abilities** (or KSAs) can help with resume building as this provides a universal language relevant for each occupation.

- **The Wage and Employment Trends** provide information about local average wages and whether this occupation is expected to increase or decrease in the number of jobs.

- The **Job Openings on the Web** identifies current employment opportunities by selecting a ZIP code, state and the website you would like to search (the most commonly used is Indeed).

3. *Discovery 7C: EXPLORING YOUR SKILLS MATCH OCCUPATION #1*

7. On the **Occupation Keyword Search** webpage with the list of occupations, select your FIRST OF TWO occupations to explore and record any useful information in the table below.

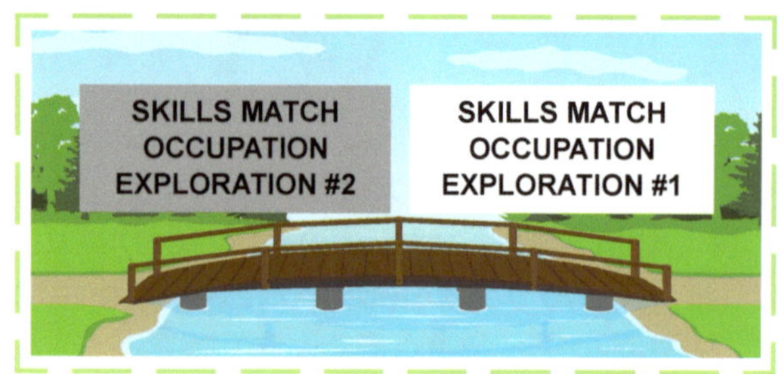

Title of Skills Occupation Match #1: ___________________________	Feel free to write in any information or notes to yourself below:
• **Sample of Reported Job Titles** • Tasks • Technology Skills • Work Activities • Detailed Work Activities • Work Context • Job Zone • Training & Credentials • Apprenticeship Opportunities • **Skills** • **Knowledge** • Education • **Abilities** • Interests • Work Values • Work Styles • **Wage and Employment Trends** • **Job Openings on the Web** • Related Occupations Additional Information	

8. To explore your **SECOND** Skills Match Occupation, look to the top right side of the webpage for **Occupation keyword search** and enter a different Skills Match from pages 38 or 39 of this Discovery-Guide. Click on **Go** and if relevant, choose an occupation to explore in more detail.

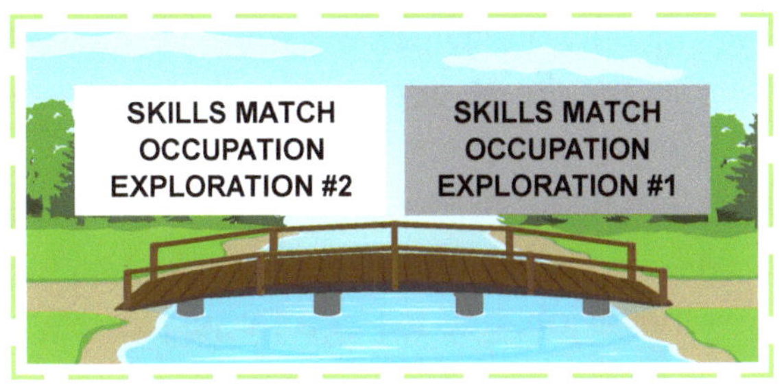

Title of Skills Occupation Match #2: ________________________	Feel free to write in any information or notes to yourself below:
• **Sample of Reported Job Titles** • Tasks • Technology Skills • Work Activities • Detailed Work Activities • Work Context • Job Zone • Training & Credentials • Apprenticeship Opportunities • **Skills** • **Knowledge** • Education • **Abilities** • Interests • Work Values • Work Styles • **Wage and Employment Trends** • **Job Openings on the Web** • Related Occupations Additional Information	

XII. A REVIEW AND CONSOLIDATION OF OUR DISCOVERY TOOLS 1-7

We will now briefly review where we have been and what tools we have explored so far, to help us maximize our job search activity.

1. **Discovery Tool 1**
   We began by identifying our priorities to consider and whether we are searching for a survival job, gap job or a target job (page 8).

▼ For Discovery Tools 2 through 5, we relied primarily on information from https://www.careeronestop.org (pages 15-31):

2. **Discovery Tools 2A-2B**
   In our second set of Discoveries, we explored our Interest Appreciation Assessment results from our RIASEC scores at careeronestop.org.

3. **Discovery Tools 3A-3C**
   We focused on translating our RIASEC results into possible Occupational Interest Career Matches.

4. **Discovery Tools 4A-4C**
   Next, we identified the Possible Occupational Skills Career Matches acquired from our past and present activities.

5. **Discovery Tools 5A-5D**
   In this set of Discoveries, we consolidated our information to review our RIASEC results, as well as refine our findings for possible Interest Matches and Skills Comparison Matches. We also identified any Interests and Skills Matches which seemed to overlap or converge towards a similar emphasis.

▼ To translate our interest and skills career matches into occupations and occupational categories, we moved to the website https://www.onetonline.org for the remaining Discovery Tools 6 and 7 (pages 35-41):

6. **Discovery 6A-6D**
   Here, we worked on translating our Interest Career Matches into occupations or occupational categories by moving to a different website focused on working with occupations (onetonline.org).

7. **Discovery 7A-7E**
   In this set of Discovery Tools, we translated our Skills Career Matches into occupations for fine-tuning our information towards possible job searches.

Our next set of occupational explorations will involve comparing two different occupations with each other. This can help us evaluate how to best decide about our future direction, which is especially useful when we have more than one occupational option to thoughtfully consider.

The section starting on the next page of this Discovery-Guide will help us compare different occupations with each other, to become even more informed about our potential options. Considering how you might creatively integrate your interests and skills may provide you with new ideas to enhance the work you enjoy doing. While many of us do find innovative ways to connect our interests and skills with each other, we can also do this by continuously exploring ways to make the work we do as meaningful as possible.

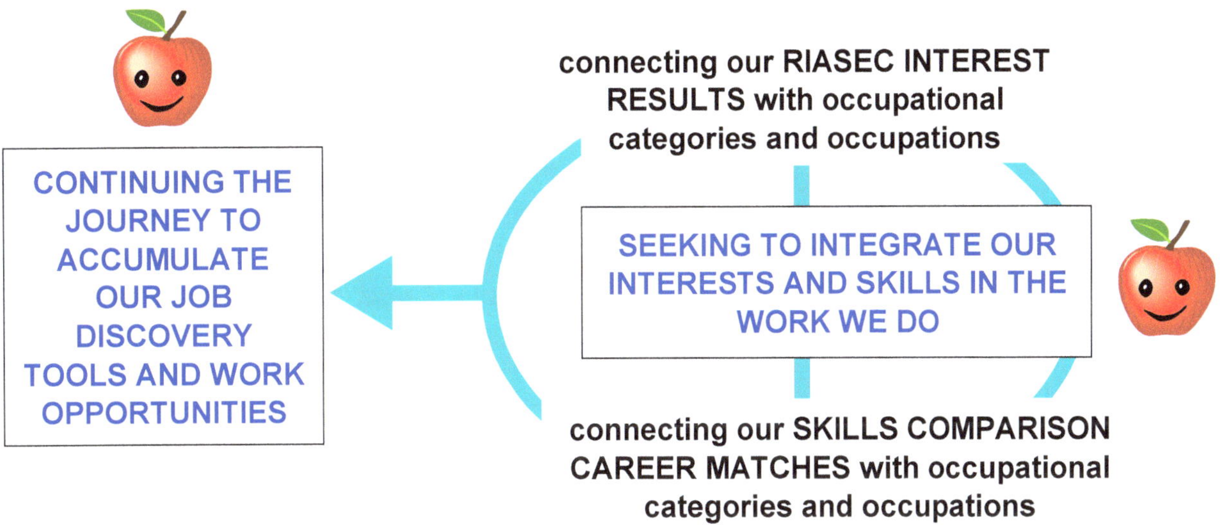

If you feel like you have been intently concentrating to help identify different ways of job searching, you have! Excellent Work! 😊

Are you ready to take another break before moving on? If yes, now would be a good time. 😊

XIII. COMPARING OCCUPATIONS IN THE JOB DISCOVERY TOOLBOX

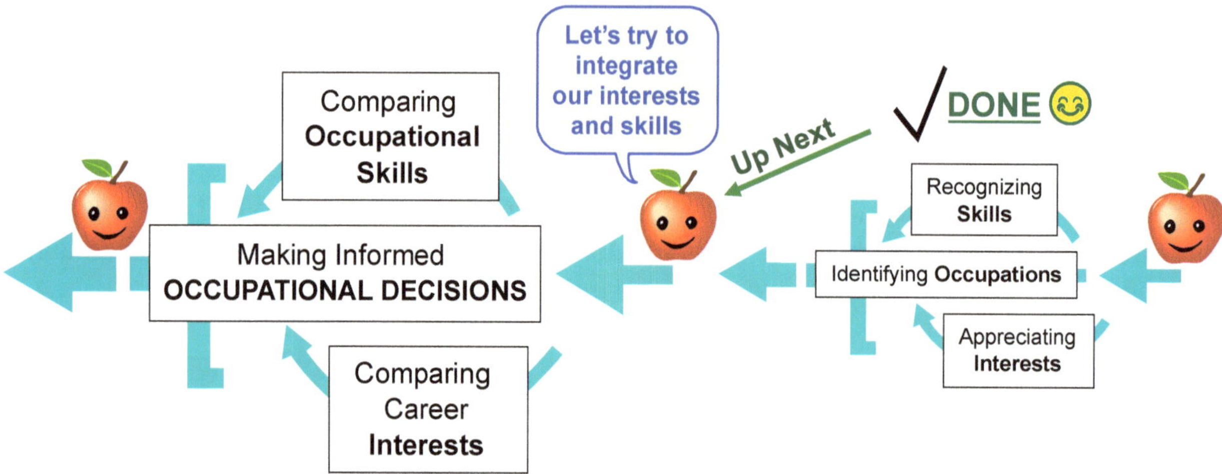

In addition to exploring individual occupations, another useful approach is to compare different occupations with each other. For example, the occupation of an office clerk shares similarities with those of a medical records clerk. Comparing these occupations with each other can help outline the similarities and differences as well as provide guidance for how to move across similar occupations and even into new industries.

In this section, we will be working across two websites again – onetonline.org and careeronestop.org – where we will translate your Career Matches into comparable occupational categories and then compare two different occupations with each other. By this time, you may have quite a few occupations to work with. However, we are initially going to work with the similar Interest and Skills Career Matches you identified earlier in this Discovery-Guide.

As a refresher, on page 31 of this Discovery-Guide (Discovery Tool 5D), you identified similar careers when comparing your Interest Assessment results and Skills Comparison Matches. This is where you wrote in the table any careers that seemed to include both your Interests and your Skills. We will first return to this and explore any two careers of your choosing for translation into occupations and then, compare these occupations with each other. Afterwards, you will have the opportunity to compare any two occupations you are interested in, from the options you have identified throughout this Discovery-Guide.

A. DISCOVERY TOOLS 8A-8C – Comparing Your Interest and Skills Career Matches

This next set of Discovery Tools will focus on comparing TWO occupations with each other. We will begin by utilizing your previous career matches, translate these into occupations, and then explore their similarities and differences.

1. Discovery 8A: SELECTING TWO CAREER MATCHES

On page 31 for **Discovery 5D** (**Your Interest Assessment and Skills Career Matches**), you may have listed two or more similar Career Matches. Select and write in at least TWO Career Matches to compare with each other.

a. **Similar Career Match #1:**	b. **Similar Career Match #2:**

c. Below, list any **other Occupational or Career Matches** you would like to compare, perhaps in the future, if time does not allow doing this now.

(As a refresher, you have identified possible Career Matches and Occupations or Occupational Categories in this Discovery-Guide on pages 18, 19, 20, 25, 27, 28, 30, 31, 35, 36, 37, 38, 39, 40 and 41.)

____

____

____

First, we are going to compare TWO of your Similar Career Matches as potential occupations. Then, you will be able to utilize one of your occupational matches listed above to find other similar occupations.

When you are ready, move to the next page and continue.

1. Go to https://www.careeronestop.org.

2. Near the top right side of the webpage in the blue horizontal bar, look for **Toolkit**. Select **Toolkit**. On the left side is a column entitled **Careers**. Below **Careers**, look down the list and click on **Compare Occupations**. This will take you to a new webpage. **Move to the next box if the website has changed.**

3. **Helpful Tip: If the website moves information around, do a search for Compare Occupations (for example) in Search CareerOneStop at the upper right of the webpage, and look for an option to Compare Occupations.**

4. On the webpage under the words **First Occupation**, **type in one of the Similar Career Matches you listed on the previous page of this Discovery-Guide.** If a menu opens, **select the most closely related occupation** from the list.

5. Under the words **Second Occupation**, **type in a second Similar Career Match you would like to compare** (from the previous page in this Discovery-Guide) and click on **Compare**. Again, if a menu opens, **select the closest occupational category** and then, click on **Compare**. This will take you to a new webpage.

6. On the **Compare Occupations** webpage, there is an option in the box on the left side to change the **Location** from the **US** to a City or State of your choosing (counties are not an option). If you would like information for a specific **City or State in the U.S.**, **type this in** and click on **Compare**. If you would like to see aggregate data for the U.S., this information is already listed below on the webpage.

Record any information of interest in the table on the next page of this Discovery-Guide.

7. You now have a side-by-side comparison of two different occupations.

8. Near the bottom, on the left side of this **Compare Occupations** webpage, is a box with the word **Download**. By selecting to **Download** as a **PDF** or **Word** document, you can then **save your results to a USB drive and/or print a copy for your records from the PDF or Word file.**

2. *Discovery 8B: COMPARING TWO CAREER MATCH OCCUPATIONS #1*

The table below provides space to write notes from comparing TWO DIFFERENT occupations.

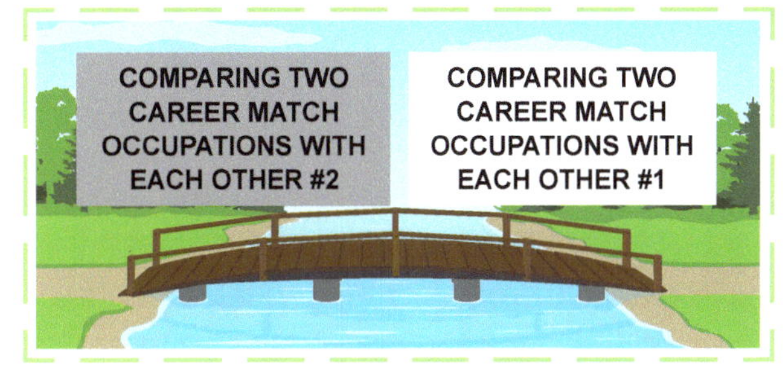

Possible Categories for Comparing These Two Different Occupations:	Title of Occupation #1:	Title of Occupation #2:
Salary		
Similar Skills and Knowledge		
Skills and Knowledge Gaps		
Employment trends		
Expected job openings		
Typical level of training (may include links to identify local training places)		
Licenses		
Certification (with the option to Find Certifications, if relevant)		
Additional notes:		

3. *Discovery 8C: COMPARING TWO CAREER MATCH OCCUPATIONS #2*

If you have another pair of occupations to compare from **Discovery 8A** on page 45, enter in your **First** and **Second** Occupations under **New Comparison** on the left side of the webpage, click **Compare**, and write your information in the table below.

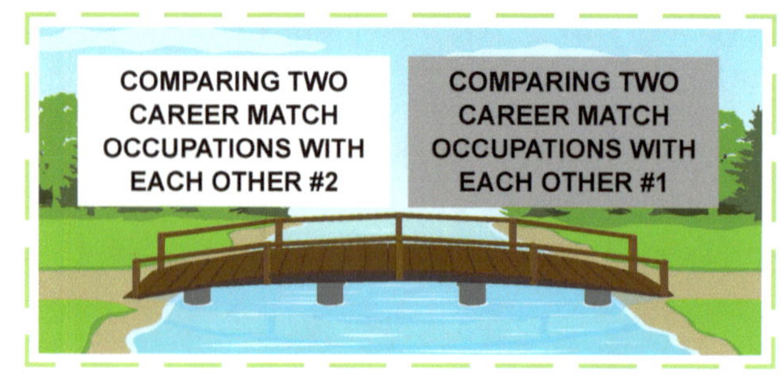

Possible Categories for Comparing These Two Different Occupations:	Title of Occupation #1:	Title of Occupation #2:
Salary		
Similar Skills and Knowledge		
Skills and Knowledge Gaps		
Employment trends		
Expected job openings		
Typical level of training (may include links to identify local training places)		
Licenses		
Certification (with the option to Find Certifications, if relevant)		
Additional notes:		

B. Utilizing One Occupation to Find Other Similar Occupations

If we take a moment to reflect, there are several different possible career and occupational options you have identified throughout this Discovery-Guide. This means you may have multiple pathways to pursue when looking for work. However, you might find some types of work identified through this Discovery-Guide are more appealing than others. For this reason, we'll next utilize one career match or occupation of your choosing to identify other closely related occupations to consider, adding one more tool into your job search repertoire.

In the previous section of this Discovery-Guide, we compared two different Interest and/or Skills Career Matches to see how they contrasted with each other. In this section, we will be looking at one occupation of your choosing to find other similar occupations for you to explore and compare. This way, if sometime in the future you discover an 'almost-the-right-fit-for-me' type of work, you will know how to:

1. Convert a job title or type of work into an occupational category by using the "Occupation Keyword Search" at onetonline.org;

2. Identify a relevant occupation;

3. Find similar additional occupations to consider; and

4. Compare the occupations you are interested in with each other.

5. Additionally, you will soon know how to utilize one occupation to identify other, similar occupations across different industries to further support your future interests and skills.

To refine and explore the areas you are most interested in, let's briefly review all of the careers and occupations you have listed and explored in this Discovery-Guide so far. Incredibly, you have possible avenues for identifying work pathways on nineteen different pages in this Discovery-Guide: pages 18, 19, 20, 24 (perhaps), 25, 27, 28, 30, 31, 35, 36, 37, 38, 39, 40, 41, 45, 47 and 48!

Let's take a moment to review your entries in this Discovery-Guide on the pages listed above. As you review the potential career and occupational pathways you have entered into this Discovery-Guide, are there any patterns, trends or anomalies you see? Do any of your possible avenues for work seem more prominent or interesting than others?

In the next section of this Discovery-Guide, we will expand our possibilities a little further. In addition, we will familiarize ourselves a little more with the Standard Occupational Classification system or SOC (first encountered on page 39 of this Discovery-Guide at onetonline.org). As types of work are categorized into occupations, every occupation is also assigned a corresponding number referred to as a SOC (commonly pronounced "sock") code. The SOC system is maintained by the U.S. Bureau of Labor Statistics and more information can be found at https://www.bls.gov/soc.

Now, let's move on to the next section!

C. DISCOVERY TOOLS 9A-9C – Comparing Similar Occupations with Each Other

In terms of your occupational discoveries, if you have any patterns, trends or anomalies when reviewing your potential career or occupational pathways, this next Discovery Tool will help identify, sort and compare your possible options. If you did not notice any specific trends or patterns, reviewing how to compare occupations with each other can still assist with evaluating your opportunities more fully, in terms of current decision-making and into the future as well.

1. DISCOVERY 9A: FINDING SIMILAR OCCUPATIONS

From reviewing pages 18, 19, 20, 24 (perhaps), 25, 27, 28, 30, 31, 35, 36, 37, 38, 39, 40, 41, 45, 47 and 48 in this Discovery-Guide, list any careers or occupations you are interested in, to identify additional similar occupational options in your job search activity.

1. ____

2. ____

3. ____

4. ____

5. ____

6. ____

7. ____

We will next explore the first of TWO careers or occupations you have listed to find additional similar occupations and expand your job search options.

1. Go to https://www.onetonline.org and look for **Occupation keyword search** in the upper right corner of the webpage.

↓

2. **Type in ONE of the Similar Career or Occupational Matches** you listed on the previous page in **Discovery Tool 9A** and click **GO**. This will bring you to a new webpage with a list of occupations. If you are on an informational webpage for the one occupational title you entered, rather than a list, record this information in the next box (step #3) and move to step #5 in this flow-chart series (you are currently on step #2).

↓

3. From the list of occupations on this next webpage, identify ONE occupation most closely matching your interests and **First, write the following information below**:

Code (SOC Code):_________________ (the XX-XXXX.00 number under Code, or under or to the left of occupational title)

Occupation Title: ____

↓

4. If there is a list of occupations on the webpage after your **Occupation Keyword Search**, **click on the Occupation you identified above**. This will take you to a new webpage with information about this occupation.

↓

5. On this next webpage with the occupational category you selected listed at the top, scroll down near the bottom to find **Related Occupations**. Choose one of the occupations listed most closely matching a category you are interested in and **Write This Information Here**:

Code (SOC Code):____________________(listed next to or under/to the left of the occupational title)

Occupation Title: ____

↓

6. We will now move to careeronestop.org to compare these two similar occupations. Go to the https://www.careeronestop.org website.

↓

7. At the top right side of the webpage, look for **Toolkit** in the blue horizontal bar. Select **Toolkit** and find the far-left column entitled **Careers**. Under **Careers** look down the list and click on **Compare Occupations**.
This will take you to a new webpage.

↓

8. Again, if the website information has been moved, use the **Search CareerOneStop** option and **enter in keywords**, such as **Compare Occupations.**

9. On this next webpage, under the words **First Occupation** type in one of the occupations you listed on the previous page of this Discovery-Guide.
If a menu opens, choose the most closely related occupation from the list.

10. You can record information from this search on the next page of this Discovery-Guide.

11. Under the words **Second Occupation** type in your second occupational choice from the previous page in this Discovery-Guide and click on Compare. Again, select the closest occupation from the list, if relevant.
This will take you to a new webpage.

12. On this next **Compare Occupations** webpage, there is an option on the left side to change the **Location** from the **US** to a City or State (counties are not an option) of your choosing. If you would like to focus on occupational information for a specific geographic area, type in a City or State in the U.S., and click on Compare. Aggregate data for the U.S. is the default search and already on this webpage. Record any information of interest on the next page of this Discovery-Guide.

13. You now have a side-by-side comparison of two different occupations and can record information in the table provided on the next page of this Discovery-Guide.

14. **To SAVE or PRINT**: Near the bottom of this webpage is a box with the word **Download**. By selecting to Download as a PDF or Word document, you can then save your results to a USB drive and/or print a copy for your records from this file.

2. *Discovery 9B: COMPARING TWO SIMILAR OCCUPATIONS #1*

The table below provides space to write notes about the TWO similar occupations.

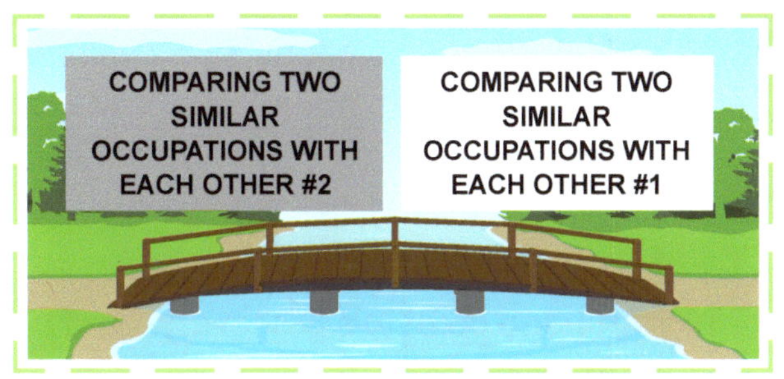

Possible Categories for Comparing These Two Similar Occupations:	Title of Occupation #1:	Title of Occupation #2:
Salary		
Similar Skills and Knowledge		
Skills and Knowledge Gaps		
Employment trends		
Expected job openings		
Typical level of training (may include links to identify local training places)		
Licenses		
Certification (with the option to Find Certifications, if relevant)		
Additional notes:		

15. The instructions on pages 51-52 will repeat to compare your Second set of similar occupations. Return to https://www.onetonline.org and look for **Occupation keyword search** in the upper right corner of the webpage.

16. **From page 50** of this Discovery-Guide in **Discovery Tool 9A, type in a Similar Career or Occupational Match** and click on **Go**. This will bring you to a new webpage with a list of occupations. If you arrive at a webpage with information for just one occupation, record this occupation in the next flow-chart box and move to step #19 in this flow-chart series.

17. Choose one of the occupations listed most closely matching the area you are interested in and **write this information below**:

Code (SOC Code):_____________________(listed near the occupational title)

Occupational Title: ____

18. If you are on a webpage with a list of occupations, **click on the Occupation you selected** (above this flow-chart box). This will take you to a new webpage with information about this occupation.

19. On this next webpage with the occupational category you selected, scroll down near the bottom to find **Related Occupations**. Choose one of the occupations you are interested in exploring from the list and **write this information here**:

Code (SOC Code): _____________________(listed next to the occupational title)

Occupational Title: ____

20. We will now move to careeronestop.org to compare these two similar occupations. Go to the https://www.careeronestop.org website.

21. At the top right side of the webpage, look for **Toolkit**. Under **Careers** on the left side, find and click on **Compare Occupations**. This will take you to a new webpage. **Again, use the Search CareerOneStop tool, if relevant.**

22. We will now compare these two similar occupations with each other. There is a table on the next page of this Discovery-Guide where you can record information.

23. Under the words **First Occupation**, type in one of the occupations you listed on the previous page of this Discovery-Guide. If a menu opens, choose the most closely related occupation from the list.

24. Under the words **Second Occupation**, type in your second occupational choice from the previous page in this Discovery-Guide and click on Compare. Again, if a menu opens, select the **closest** occupation, and then click on Compare. This will take you to a new webpage.

25. On the **Compare Occupations** webpage, there is an option in the box on the left side to change the **Location** from the **US** to a preferred City or State of your choosing. If you would like to focus on occupational information for a specific City or State in the U.S., type this in and click on Compare. If you would like to see aggregate **data for the U.S.**, this is already listed on the webpage.

Record any information of interest on the next page of this Discovery-Guide.

26. You now have a side-by-side comparison of two different occupations and can record information in the table provided on the next page of this Discovery-Guide.

27. **To SAVE or PRINT:** Near the bottom of this webpage is a box with the word **DOWNLOAD**. By selecting to Download as a PDF or Word document, you can then save your results to a USB drive and/or print a copy for your records.

3. *Discovery 9C: COMPARING TWO SIMILAR OCCUPATIONS #2*

Record your information of interest about the TWO occupations in the table below.

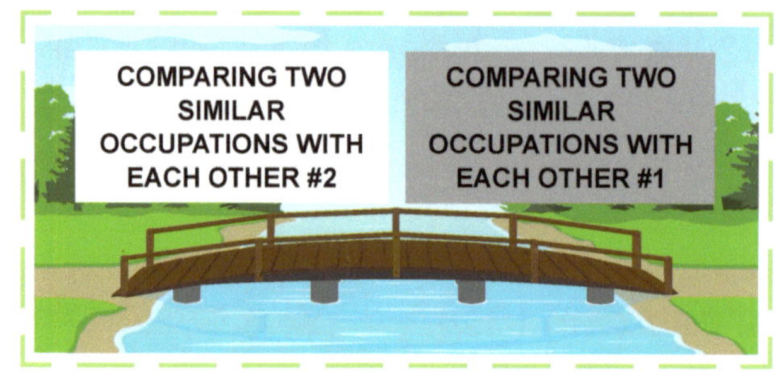

Possible Categories for Comparing These Two Similar Occupations:	Title of Occupation #1:	Title of Occupation #2:
Salary		
Similar Skills and Knowledge		
Skills and Knowledge Gaps		
Employment trends		
Expected job openings		
Typical level of training (may include links to identify local training places)		
Licenses		
Certification (with the option to Find Certifications, if relevant)		
Additional notes:		

CONGRATULATIONS AGAIN! We are almost through all of the Discoveries in this Discovery-Guide!

You now have a number of different Discovery Tools to help you to explore and find the kind of work you want to do. 😊

However, there are two final tools we will investigate before completing our Discovery-Guide activities:

1. How to anticipate the potential longer-term stability offered by your next job or future work; and

2. If an industry does not have many available jobs, how to find other industries with similar occupations relevant to your interests and skills.

If you would like to refresh your attention and take a moment to contemplate what you are discovering, now might be a great time to do this before proceeding to the next section, as we will be transitioning into a new topic of Discovery. 😊

XIV. EXPLORING THE CURRENT AND FUTURE OUTLOOK OF AN OCCUPATION

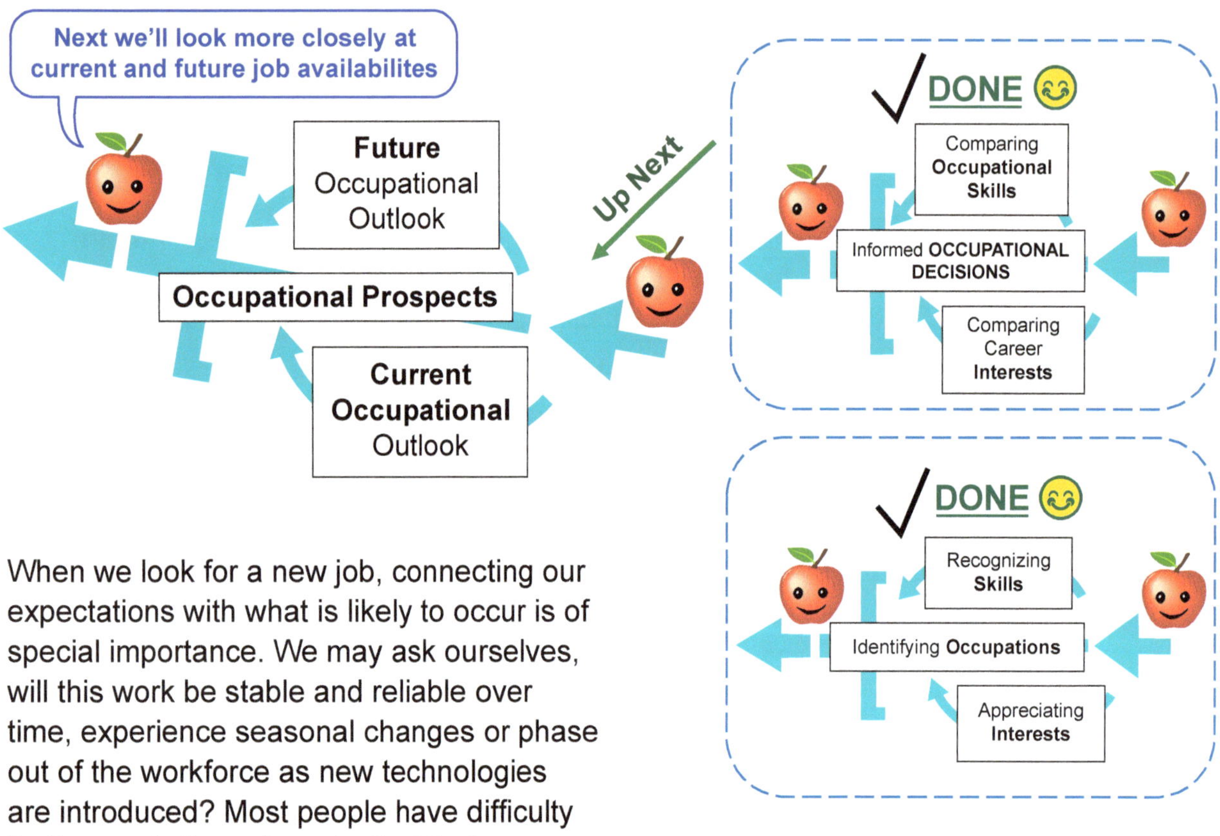

When we look for a new job, connecting our expectations with what is likely to occur is of special importance. We may ask ourselves, will this work be stable and reliable over time, experience seasonal changes or phase out of the workforce as new technologies are introduced? Most people have difficulty finding work *through no fault of their own*, but because jobs are related to what economists refer to as a supply and demand in the workforce. From this perspective, all jobs exist within a labor market or labor markets, meaning there is a supply and demand for different types of workers, and at different times, to fill positions with employers.

> For example, when restaurants closed during the beginning of the Covid-19 (2020) pandemic, many, many restaurant workers could not find employment because restaurants were not hiring. In fact, restaurants were laying off workers because they could not pay wages. This is an extreme example of a low demand (or no demand) for restaurant workers by employers, and a high supply of potential restaurant employees. However, this type of phenomenon, although usually less extreme, is continuously occurring with many different types of jobs in the labor market.

For this reason, the U.S. Department of Labor (through the Bureau of Labor Statistics) collects data and information on which occupations are increasing, remaining stable or declining and based on this information, provides predictions on the future outlook for the different occupations. In addition, following trends about what kinds of decisions employers are making such as moving more towards automation or relying more on the skills of people, can help inform us about the future too. If interested, you can find more information at the Bureau of Labor Statistics website, https://www.bls.gov/ooh, where the latest data from their Occupational Outlook Handbook (OOH) is available. This website is also listed in Appendix B: Glossary of Terms, located at the end of this Discovery-Guide.

While the Occupational Outlook Handbook looks at trends mostly across the U.S. in aggregate, in the next part of this Discovery-Guide we will also be looking at trends focused towards our local regions, since this information is most relevant when considering where we plan to live and work.

A. Looking at Occupational Trends in Your City, County or State

All states and many large counties keep track of whether the demand for different occupations is rising, declining or staying the same. Some larger cities might do this too, if there is enough funding available to collect and maintain data on local labor markets. In addition, the Bureau of Labor Statistics as well as the Census Bureau collects information across the nation to assist with providing future projections as accurately as possible.

Looking at labor market information pertinent to where we live can help inform and anticipate what might be occurring, especially during the next few years and further into the future. Information about the outlook of an occupation can help us anticipate the amount of change we may experience with the type of work we are (or will be) doing and about the industry we are (or might be) working in.

The next pages of this Discovery-Guide will assist us with looking at regional and county information for Washington State. If this is not the geographic area you are interested in, follow the flow-chart on the right side of the next page for suggestions on other states and counties. Since most states collect and present their data differently, finding information about the trends for different types of occupations will be unique to each geographic location. Usually, there is a state website linked with unemployment insurance information where the supply and demand for jobs can be located.

If, after following the flow-chart, such information does not seem readily available, try calling or sending an email to the state's unemployment or labor department. Try asking for a website address to find the supply and demand for different occupations in the state and/ or county you are looking for, and they should be able to help.

Ready to begin? Let's move to the next page.

For Washington State

1a. Do an internet search for **Washington State occupations in demand**. Select the **Occupations in Demand list** at: https://esd.wa.gov/labormarketinfo/learn-about-an-occupation#/search. This internet search is useful in case ESD (Employment Security Department) changes the webpage address.

1b. You will be at a webpage with a list of all occupations in Washington State listed by **SOC#**, the Standard Occupational Classification numbering system as designated by the Bureau of Labor Statistics. This list is NOT in order from highest to lowest in Demand, but is from the lowest to highest SOC code.

1c. In the heading of the table look for:

Instead of **Displaying 100 of the current total**, click on the down arrow and **change the 100 to 1000**. This will display all of the occupations listed on one webpage.

For Other States and Counties

OR

2a. Do an internet search for the **state or county** you are interested in, followed by **occupations in demand**. Some states have more information than others, so search down the results list to see if your state of interest has a website listed (**look for or search with a .gov extension**) and go to this website, or there might be a different website listed. If you cannot find relevant information, go to the next step at 2b.

2b. If you cannot find any information about the State you are interested in, all states are required to collect labor market information and you can find your State's website at: https://www.bls.gov/bls/ofolist.htm.

Go to this website and look on the list provided for the State you are interested in.

2c. At https://www.bls.gov/bls/ofolist.htm, look down the list to find the State you are interested in and **click on the link provided for Internet.** This link will take you to the State's employment information homepage.

Move to the next page of this Discovery-Guide.

For Washington State

1d. On the far-left side of the table is the word **Demand**. By clicking on Demand once, the list will re-sort.

First on this new list will be occupations with unchanging demand, then occupations in decline, and at the end of the list will be occupations increasing in demand as denoted by the direction of the arrows in the column rows.

1e. By clicking on the word Demand a second time, the list will re-sort to show the occupations in demand first, the occupations in decline next and those remaining unchanged last.

1f. Clicking on the Occupation Title **in the table heading twice** will change the list to be in alphabetical order (from A-Z) so you can find a specific occupational title more easily.

OR

For Other States and Counties

2d. Since every State provides information differently on their website, look on the homepage to see if there are keywords like occupations in demand or decline, occupational outlook, fastest growing jobs or occupational trends.

2e. You can also look for a search option and experiment with keywords such as occupations or jobs in demand, occupational outlook or occupational projections, to see if this will yield relevant information about the current or future jobs outlook.

2f. If you are able to find this information, move to the next box in this flow-chart. If not, you can try contacting the labor department for the state you are interested in, and ask for instructions on how to find current occupations in demand and decline.

3. Occupations **in-demand**, **balanced** or **in-decline** describe the likelihood of finding available jobs: in-demand occupations (with a green up arrow) have a high probability, balanced (with a horizontal arrow) a lesser one and in-decline (a down arrow) the lowest likelihood. This does not necessarily mean jobs cannot be found in a specific occupation, but rather, designates the total number of jobs available as higher or lower. Also useful to note is funding for training support generally requires an occupation to be **in-demand**.

You can record any information of interest from this section on the next page of this Discovery-Guide.

B. DISCOVERY TOOLS 10A-10C – Investigating Occupational Trends

This next set of Discovery Tools will help us become more informed about first, the current outlook for a job and next, the anticipated future stability for the occupations and jobs we are interested in. This can help us anticipate how likely (or not likely) a specific occupation might remain stable, increase in availability, or decline in the job market now, and into the future. Important to remember is how this information can change from unanticipated circumstances such as supply shortages impacting international trade, or because of new developments with evolving technology. For these reasons, you can periodically check to see how an occupational outlook might be changing over time.

Included in the Discovery table below are SOC codes from the Standard Occupational Classification system mentioned earlier (page 49). The 2018 SOC codes are periodically updated and include 867 different occupations within 459 broad categories, combined into 98 minor groups and then condensed into 23 major groupings. Imagine the amount of detailed effort required to identify and categorize the many different occupations in the U.S.! Just by knowing the first two or three SOC code numbers allows for an occupational search strategy (ahead on page 72 is a Handy Search Tip to try this out). A full list of SOC categories can be found at: https://www.bls.gov/soc/2018/major_groups.htm or by going to https://www.bls.gov and doing a search for **SOC occupations**. Onetonline.org does utilize SOC codes (as does Washington State). However, not all of the websites we are visiting will.

Later in this Discovery-Guide, we will explore more detailed information about the current and future outlooks of specific occupations, as well as become more familiar with SOC codes.

1. *Discovery 10A: IDENTIFYING SPECIFIC OCCUPATIONAL TITLES*

Write your occupations of interest in the table below from the website(s) found while following the flow-chart (for Washington State or a different State) on the previous page of this Discovery-Guide.

Code (SOC)	Occupational Title	Location (if relevant)	Currently In Demand, Decline or the Same? (if available)	Notes for Additional Information
1.				
2.				
3.				
4.				

Great work! Next, we will resume working through the flow-chart on the next page.

For Washington StateFor Other States and Counties

4a. At the esd.wa.gov webpage listing occupations in-demand, balanced and in-decline, click on a **specific Occupational Title** to open a webpage with more detailed information.

OR

5a. If you were able to find a list of occupations at a website for your State of interest, try clicking on the occupational title to see if more information is available about that occupation.

If you are unable to find more information, move to the next step in this flow-chart.

4b. The information on this webpage is entitled **Learn about an occupation**. Scroll down to find information such as **Job description, Education and training, Pay, Employment trends**, etc. At the bottom right side of this webpage, look for **Explore Careers**. Below this, clicking on **CareerOneStop** will take you to this website. The esd.wa.gov window will remain an open tab for you to return to, as needed.

5b. Since occupations in-demand, balanced or in-decline can vary from state to state and county to county, another useful option is to look at national level information. The next steps in this flow-chart will help with national level occupational outlooks.

6. If you are not already at the website, go to https://www.careeronestop.org.

7. At careeronestop.org, look in the upper right corner of the homepage for a small box with the search icon (magnifying glass). **Enter one of your occupational titles from the previous esd.wa.gov website or from page 62 of this Discovery-Guide.** (Or you can enter one of the occupations of interest you identified from the previous Discovery Tools.) Click on the **search icon** or hit the enter key on your keyboard. This will take you to a new webpage.

8. This next webpage provides information about the specific occupational title you entered. In the box entitled **We found an occupation that matches your search**, find the heading **Looking for career information?**. Look a few lines below and click on **Learn more about this career**. This will take you to a new webpage.

9. On this next **Occupational Profile** webpage, look down on the left side and near the second or third heading and you will see **Outlook: will there be jobs?**. This section will inform you about the future outlook for this occupation. You can explore any other occupations of interest to see if the future outlook influences your work preferences. **Record information about current and future job outlooks on the next page of this Discovery-Guide.**

2. *Discovery 10B: IDENTIFYING THE CURRENT AND EXPECTED FUTURE OUTLOOK OF DIFFERENT OCCUPATIONS*

While the previous Discovery Tool focused on current occupational conditions, the table below adds a column to record the anticipated future expectation or projection of an occupation. This will assist with seeing if the current *and* future demand informs you about the kind of work you would like to consider or expand on. You

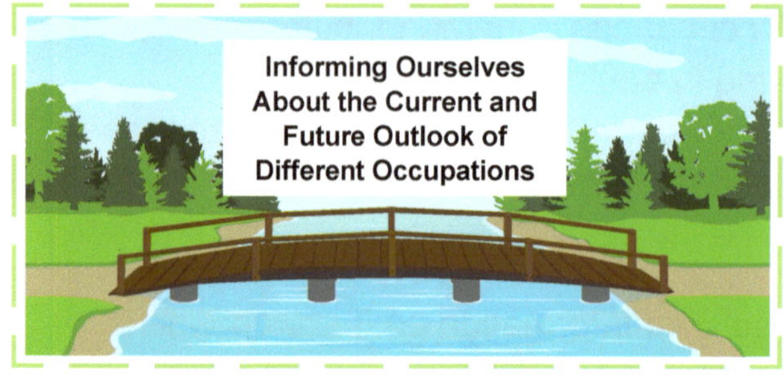

can copy the information from the previous table and add in the future projection, as well as investigate other occupations of interest. Please record your information below for FOUR occupations.

(SOC) Code (at onetonline.org or bls.gov)	Occupational Title	Currently In Demand, About the Same or In-Decline?	Future Outlook: will there be jobs? Bright (in-demand), Average (saying the same) or Below Average (in-decline)?
1.			
		Additional Notes:	
2.			
		Additional Notes:	
3.			
		Additional Notes:	
4.			
		Additional Notes:	

Excellent Work! Next we will explore occupational outlooks a little further.

C. Additional Occupational Outlook Information with the Bureau of Labor Statistics

More information about occupational outlooks is available with the U.S. Bureau of Labor Statistics. The Bureau of Labor Statistics provides access to the Occupational Outlook Handbook referred to earlier in this Discovery-Guide. Additionally, there are publications and articles on different occupations available at this website. Follow the flow-chart below to explore occupational outlook information provided by the Bureau of Labor Statistics.

1. More information on occupational outlooks can be found at the Occupational Outlook Handbook website by the Bureau of Labor Statistics. Go to their website at https://www.bls.gov/ooh.

2. Directly above the words **Occupational Outlook Handbook** are links. Click on OCCUPATION FINDER and this will take you to a list of occupations. Next, **click on the Occupation title you are interested in** from the list, and move to step #4 in this flow-chart. If you cannot find the occupation you are looking for, or if this webpage has changed, move to step #3 in this flow-chart.

The occupations are listed in alphabetical order. **You can change the number of entries per page** (above the list) or select the Next option on the upper right side, to move to the next webpage.

3. In the **Search Handbook** box, type in your occupation of interest and select Go. Here you will find more information about occupational outlooks. Find the specific occupation you are looking for and click on it. If useful, you can also review the full list of occupations in OOH by going to the **OOH SITE MAP** above the **OCCUPATIONAL OUTLOOK HANDBOOK** heading.

4. If you look down this summary webpage of a specific occupation, across the tabs at the top you will see an option (on the right side) for **Similar Occupations** (based on SOC categories). Click on Similar Occupations and this will open a webpage with a list of possible similar occupations, perhaps with different current and future job outlooks.

5. You can record any information of interest in the table on the next page of this Discovery-Guide.

1. *Discovery 10C: COMPARING THE CURRENT AND FUTURE OUTLOOK FOR DIFFERENT OCCUPATIONS*

In the table below, list any relevant information about your occupations of interest based on the information you are accumulating.

(SOC) Code (at onetonline.org)	Occupational Title	Notes and Reminders
1.		
2.		
3.		
4.		
5.		

CONGRATULATIONS! You are now familiar with several different approaches for exploring occupational outlooks. **GREAT WORK**!

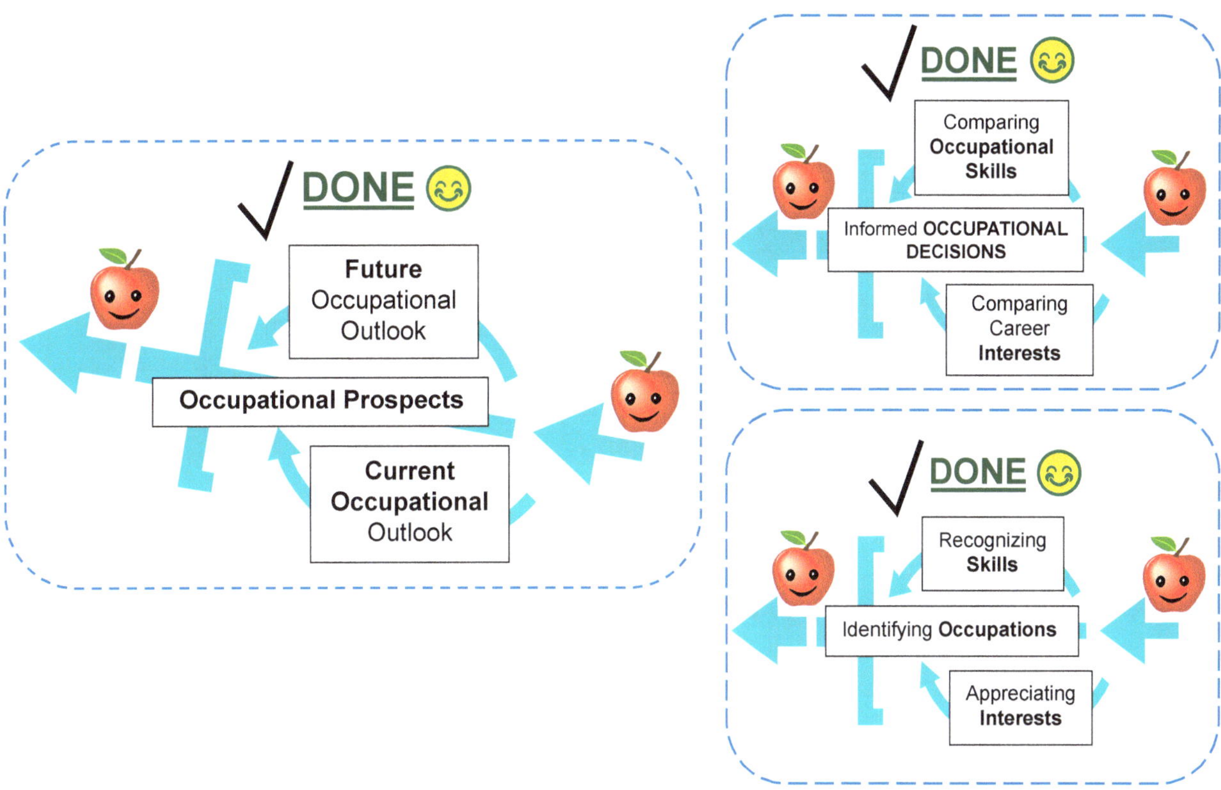

In the next set of Discovery Tools, we will introduce and focus on a series of approaches for exploring similar occupations across different INDUSTRIES. This way, we will be able to see how the type of work we do, or would like to do, can also be relevant across different industries. To conclude, the final set of Discovery Tools will offer an approach for finding job postings and if relevant, training or certification programs, for your occupations of interest identified through this Discovery-Guide.

Ready for a break to refresh before we move on? If yes, now might be a good time to pause on the Discovery-Guide before we move into the next section, where we will be working with OCCUPATIONS AND INDUSTRIES. 😊

XV. EXPLORING DIFFERENT INDUSTRIES TO DISCOVER RELATED OCCUPATIONS

As a memory refresher, the companies, organizations and businesses where we work are also categorized into different industries. In fact, there is a categorization method referred to as the North American Industry Classification System, or NAICS. The NAICS was developed jointly by Canada, Mexico and the U.S. in an attempt to standardize the categorization of all the different economic activity occurring across the North American continent – an incredibly complex undertaking requiring continuous maintenance and modification. (More information about the NAICS can be found at: https://www.census.gov/naics. Click on the **History** link near the top left of the webpage for more historical information).

In the NAICS, similar types of economic activity are grouped together under a specific industry topic, such as in the industries of construction, manufacturing, service or public administration (government). And, within each industry are sub-categories, all with associated numerical codes. Just as occupations are assigned numerical codes through the Standardized Occupational Classification system or SOC (described earlier in this Discovery-Guide on pages 49 and 62), industries and their sub-categories are assigned code numbers as well. Amazingly, the latest 2022 NAICS includes 1,012 industries on the North American continent. (More information can be found at: https://www.census.gov/naics. Click on **FAQs** at the top of the webpage for answers to common questions, or you can select the **2022 NAICS Manual** at the bottom left of the webpage to view a list of current coding categories.)

Fortunately for us, the NAICS classification system is relied upon for collecting, analyzing and publishing statistical data about economic activity in the United States. We can utilize this information to help us link different industries with occupational information. This way, we will be able to explore and discover:

1. The fastest growing *industries* with occupations similar to ones we are interested in, and

2. Similar kinds of occupations across different types of industries.

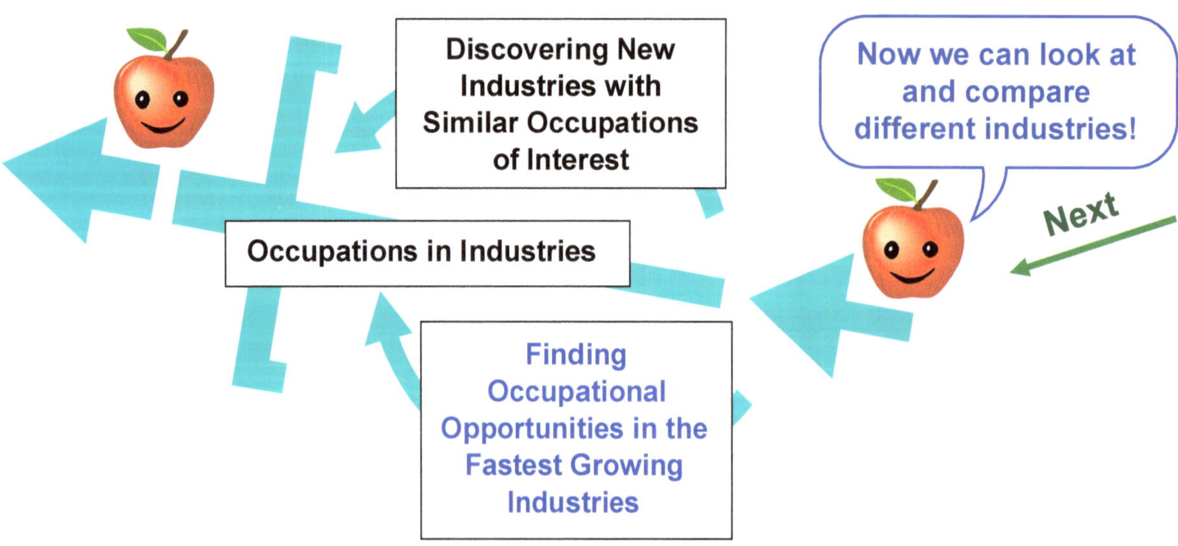

Exploring our occupational opportunities by discovering the different industries we might be interested in offers yet another approach to expand, identify and access additional work prospects.

> For example, during a time when the construction industry was in severe decline, a construction marketing representative was laid off. The company he worked for could not afford to pay him any longer – this business was trying to survive a significant downturn in customers. Given the entire industry was declining and contracting, other job openings for a construction marketing representative did not exist. However, the construction marketing representative discovered the skills he utilized were also relevant in the health care industry, as a pharmaceutical marketing representative – an industry expected to grow for many years into the future.

As the scenario above illustrates, exploring different industries for similar occupations is another way to expand our search for the type of work we want to do. By opening our activity to explore different types of industries also allows us to consider other subject areas we might enjoy learning more about.

Since all industries share an underlying common knowledge-base about their products or services, we can consider learning about new and different topics. For example, the industry category of Utilities includes the sub-category of Solar Electric Power Generation, commonly known as utilizing solar energy converted from the sun into electricity. Renewable solar energy can have many uses from small individual lamps lighting pathways in a garden, to panels on a rooftop generating heat in a home or building. Perhaps someday, more airplanes will rely on solar power instead of fossil fuels. If you have discovered a new subject area of interest, entering a related industry can offer an engaging way to learn about a different topic.

Different industries are somewhat categorized by similar subject areas linked to what a product or service is designed to address. For example, solar energy is identified as a "Utility" because electrical energy is the product being supplied – whether to a lamp, home, building or airplane. In addition, the NAICS industry categories can also serve to help us identify different subject areas where our occupational interests might fit in.

In our next Discovery Tool, we will focus on finding occupations within the fastest growing industries. The assumption is, by looking at the fastest growing industries, we are provided clues as to where more jobs can be found in a changing economic landscape.

For the next part of this Discovery-Guide, we will be working across several different websites throughout. Be sure to keep track and follow along with the flow-charts provided, as well as write the information you are gathering in each of the Discovery Tool activities.

When you are ready to begin, move to the next page and we will start our exploration into the FIRST of TWO Discoveries on different industries and their corresponding occupational opportunities. 😊

A. DISCOVERY TOOLS 11A-11F – Exploring Occupations of Interest in the Fastest Growing Industries

1. Go to https://www.careeronestop.org.

2. In the search box at the top right side of the homepage with the words **Search CareerOneStop**, type in the words **fastest growing industries** and click on the **search icon**. This will bring you to a new webpage.

3. On the webpage entitled **Fastest-Growing Industries** look just above the table with the list of industries for the sentence **We found __ growing industries in the United States**. This informs you of how many industries are listed in this search.

4. Below the table with the list of industries on this webpage and above the word **Download** is a box with **10 Per Page**. This provides an option to change the number of industries listed on a single webpage. Click on the **down arrow next to 10** and change the number of entries from **10 to 500** (500 per webpage) to see the full list on single webpage. The webpage will automatically refresh to list the fastest growing industries (for easier viewing).

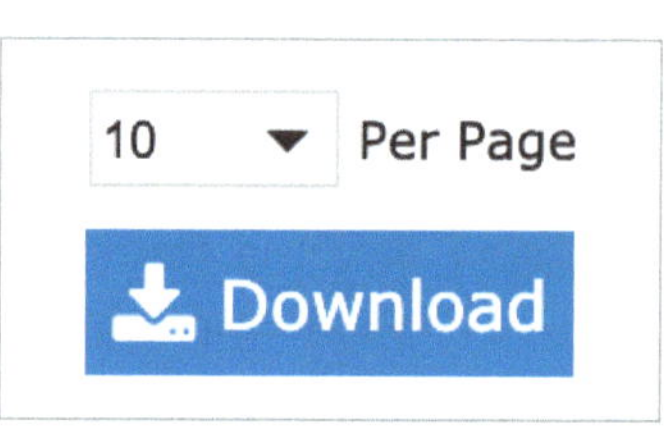

5. In the next Discovery Tool, you will be moving across different websites and recording the information you gather in the same Discovery activity table.

6. From the careeronestop.org list of **Fastest Growing Industries**, **select ONE industry and write this in the table on the next page of this Discovery-Guide**. On the webpage, when you **click on the industry you are interested in exploring**, a new window tab will open on your computer screen. Here, you will be taken to a different website by the Bureau of Labor Statistics (bls.gov). The careeronestop.org window will remain as an open internet tab for moving back and forth between these two websites.

7. Move to the next page of this Discovery-Guide to begin **Discovery 11A:** Identifying Relevant Occupations in Different Industries of Interest.

1. *Discovery 11A: IDENTIFYING POTENTIAL OCCUPATIONS IN DIFFERENT INDUSTRIES OF INTEREST*

Record your information from the two different websites – careeronestop.org and bls.gov – in the table below. Select at least TWO different industries to explore.

<table>
<tr><td>8a. From the **Fastest Growing Industries** list at careeronestop.org, **select an Industry you find interesting to explore and write this in the table below**. On the webpage, **click on this Industry**. A new window tab will open at **bls.gov**. Move to the next step in this flow-chart to the right of this box.</td><td>8b. The **Industry at a Glance** webpage with **bls.gov** provides an overview of this industry's activities. Scroll down past a few tables to the heading **Employment by Occupation**. Write in any occupations of interest in the table below. We will explore these occupations more fully in our next Discovery activity.</td></tr>
</table>

8c. **Return to steps #8a (this window tab is still open) and #8b above to repeat exploring different industry occupations.** The table below provides space for up to four different industries. When finished, move to the next page of this Discovery-Guide.

From the list of Fastest Growing Industries, **write in up to Four Industries below**.	At **bls.gov** Industries at a Glance, **write down your Occupations of Interest below**.
1.	1a.
	1b.
2.	2a.
	2b.
3.	3a.
	3b.
4.	4a.
	4b.

We will now move to onetonline.org and explore further, the occupations you have identified.

9. Go to https://www.onetonline.org.

10. In the **Occupation keyword search** box located at the top right of the webpage, **type in one of the OCCUPATIONS you identified from the previous Discovery 11A** activity on page 71 and click on **Go**, if relevant. This will take you to a new webpage with information about this occupation.

11. If relevant, click on your Occupation of interest for more information about this industry-based occupation. **Below the occupation title at the top left of the webpage is a corresponding SOC CODE and below this, a job description. Below these, look for the words** **Sample of reported job titles**. For your information, this is a list of job titles different employers identified for this occupational category.

On the next Discovery-Guide pages, you will be able to record information for up to THREE occupations from your list on the previous page of this Discovery-Guide.

12. Move to the next page of this Discovery-Guide to record information about your selected industry-related occupation(s). **After investigating your first occupation, return to the** **Occupation keyword search** **box at onetonline.org (look to the upper right corner of the webpage) and explore two additional occupations**.

Try this Handy Search TIP with **Discovery 11D** on page 75 in this Discovery-Guide!

Handy Search TIP – Here's a helpful tip when exploring occupations in industries:

1. At www.onetonline.org, in the **Occupation keyword search** box at the upper right corner, **type in the first two numbers of a SOC code followed by a dash (-)**: For example, **35-** will highlight food preparation and service occupations or **47-** will provide a list of construction and extraction occupations.

For a more specific list, enter the first two numbers followed by a dash (-), and then the third number. (Example: 35-2 for food preparation.)

2. After entering either the first two or three numbers of a SOC code, **click on the arrow** to see a list of related occupations! You can try this in **Discovery 11D**.

2. *Discovery 11B: EXPLORING OCCUPATIONS IN A GROWING INDUSTRY #1*

In the table below, record your information of interest for ONE industry occupation in the **Occupation keyword search**.

Title of Industry #1: ____

Title of Occupation #1:____

SOC Code:____________________	Relevant Information and Notes:
• **Sample of Reported Job Titles** • Tasks • Technology Skills • Work Activities • Detailed Work Activities • Work Context • Job Zone • Training & Credentials • Apprenticeship Opportunities • **Skills** • **Knowledge** • Education • **Abilities** • Interests • Work Values • Work Styles • **Wage and Employment Trends** • **Job Openings on the Web** • Related Occupations Additional Information	

3. *Discovery 11C: EXPLORING OCCUPATIONS IN A GROWING INDUSTRY #2*

In the table below, record information for a SECOND industry occupation (from page 71) in the **Occupation keyword search at onetonline.org**.

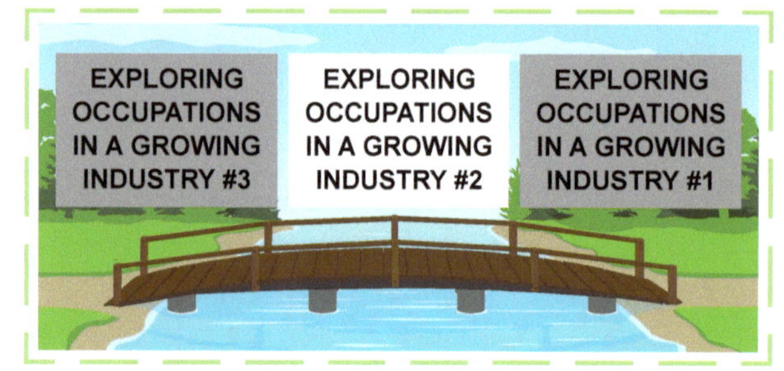

Title of Industry #2: ____

Title of Occupation #2:____

SOC Code:_____________________	Relevant Information and Notes:
• **Sample of Reported Job Titles**	
• Tasks	
• Technology Skills	
• Work Activities	
• Detailed Work Activities	
• Work Context	
• Job Zone	
• Training & Credentials	
• Apprenticeship Opportunities	
• **Skills**	
• **Knowledge**	
• Education	
• **Abilities**	
• Interests	
• Work Values	
• Work Styles	
• **Wage and Employment Trends**	
• **Job Openings on the Web**	
• Related Occupations	
Additional Information	

4. Discovery 11D:
EXPLORING OCCUPATIONS IN A GROWING INDUSTRY #3

In the table below, record your information of interest for a THIRD industry and corresponding occupation of interest.

Title of Industry #3: ____

Title of Occupation #3:____

SOC Code:___________________	Relevant Information and Notes:
• **Sample of Reported Job Titles**	
• Tasks	
• Technology Skills	
• Work Activities	
• Detailed Work Activities	
• Work Context	
• Job Zone	
• Training & Credentials	
• Apprenticeship Opportunities	
• **Skills**	
• **Knowledge**	
• Education	
• **Abilities**	
• Interests	
• Work Values	
• Work Styles	
• **Wage and Employment Trends**	
• **Job Openings on the Web**	
• Related Occupations	
Additional Information	

B. Reviewing Industry and Employment Trends of Interest in Your State

In addition to our previous industry explorations, confirming information about the fastest growing industries in a specific State can be useful for gaining insights about a particular geographic region. This search may be a little more complicated, since each State organizes their information differently. In addition, some States may offer reports to read or provide data in Microsoft Excel spreadsheets, so you may need to have Excel (or an Excel compatible format) to view more detailed local industry trends.

Feel free to move to the next Discovery-Guide section on page 79, if you prefer to return to this at a later time. Remember too, you might be able to contact your state's unemployment office to request assistance with finding local industry trends.

For Washington State

1a. Do an internet search for **industry projections Washington State** and select or go to: https://www.esd.wa.gov/labormarketinfo/projections. (The website address is often identified above the search title.)

If the information location has changed, do a search at the esd.wa.gov website for **labor market info**. Then click on the heading **Labor market info** to access their homepage at: https://esd.wa.gov/labormarketinfo. Under the **Labor market menu** on the left side column, look down the list for the heading **EMPLOYMENT** and click on **Projections**. This should take you to a webpage entitled **Projections** (in orange letters near the top). If the webpage has changed, do **a search for labor market projections**.

1b. On the **Projections** webpage, scroll down to the very bottom until you see a box entitled **Industry employment projections**. Within the box is a table entitled **Industry employment projections (2, 5 and 10 year forecast)**.

For Other States

2a. Do an internet search for **fastest growing industries** or **industry projections** and the **State** you are interested in.

2b. Look at your search results for a link to the State's employment department with a .gov extension (instead of a .com) or include a **.gov** in your keyword search. Go to this website and look to see if there are any reports or tables on industries in the state.

2c. **YES** – If you locate industry information from a state government website, or a different website (you can check your search to see if there are other options for industry information), move to the next Discovery-Guide page to record information.

2d. **NO** – If you do not find information on industries for the State you are interested in, you can try calling the state employment office or send an email to request instructions on how to locate this information.

1c. If useful, above the words **Industry employment** projections (2, 5 and 10 year forecast) are options to **Select an Area/Workforce Development Area** and **Select an Industry Sector** from the drop-down menu of items. The table will automatically change to reflect your selections.

1d. Use the side and bottom scroll bars to move up, down, right or left on the table view. The list of projections are in alphabetical order by industry and show 2, 5 and 10 year forecasts for the number of individuals employed as well as in percent. Look across the top of the table headings for column descriptions.

2e.

YES
Move to the
Discovery 11E
below to record your
information of interest.

NO
Move to page 79
of this Discovery-
Guide in preparation
for exploring a new
website in the
next section.

1. *Discovery 11E: EXPLORING STATE AND LOCAL INDUSTRY GROWTH PROJECTIONS*

In the table below, record any information of interest from the **Industry employment projections**.

Write in your **industries of interest** below.	Write in any notes about **current data, future projections or comparisons with national data** from **Discoveries 11A-11D**.
1.	
2.	
3.	
4.	
5. Additional Information, perhaps from the activity on the next page of this Discovery-Guide.	

If you are interested in exploring the industry projections further for Washington State and have Microsoft Excel, follow along with the flow-chart below. If you are viewing labor market information in a Microsoft Excel format for a different State, go to box 1e in the flow-chart on this page and follow along to see if any of the suggestions are useful. Or, you can move to the next page of this Discovery-Guide.

1e. **Above the Industry Employment Projections box** are lists of more in-depth information. Look for the title **Industry projections** (with the current year) by scrolling above the box we've been exploring in.

1f. Under the Industry projections title are data files you can download into an Excel spreadsheet for:

Short-term industry projections

Long-term industry projections

All industry projections

Click on the file of your choosing to view the data. This will open a Microsoft Excel spreadsheet on your computer.

1g. The downloaded Excel spreadsheet (after selecting from the webpage list) will provide a table with different geographic areas to choose from. Click on the area of your choosing and this will open another file with area-specific data.

1h. If you are familiar with Excel, you can enable the editing function and sort the data. In the Excel file, click on one of the titles to identify the row you are interested in. Then, go to Data and click on Sort to open a window where you can select the field and order of the sorting from a drop-down menu. (For the Washington State Data, the sorting process may re-sort the sub-headings and re-arrange the headings, so you may need to remember the industry heading as well.)

If you prefer to view the table as is, one suggestion is to look for the rates of industry growth to see if an industry you are interested in is projected to grow, stay the same or not. Also useful is to see if the State level information is consistent with the national data we reviewed in the previous Discovery Tools 11A-11D.

You can add any information of interest into the table on the previous page of this Discovery-Guide.

1i. When you are finished with your State industry explorations, move to the next page of this Discovery-Guide.

2. *Discovery 11F: EXPLORING CURRENT STATE AND LOCAL EMPLOYMENT INFORMATION*

While being aware of *future projections* for industries and occupations is important, reviewing *current trends* is also useful. This way, we can be more informed not only about the future outlook, but also about current prospects for the work we are interested in. For this reason, we will take a very brief excursion to include current employment, wages and other trends for the state or locality where you are planning to work.

> 1. Go to https://www.bls.gov and look for the blue bar across the top for the heading **SUBJECTS**.

> 2. Click on the **arrow next to SUBJECTS** and a box will open. In the middle column, look for heading **Employment** and under this, click on **State and Local Employment**.

> 3. On this next webpage entitled **State and Metro Area Employment, Hours and Earnings**, scroll down to the very bottom right side for **State and Area Resources**. In the map, **click on your State of interest** and this will open a new webpage with a list of available information by State.

> 4. This next webpage is entitled **Geographic Information** (at the top). **Locate your State of Interest** and then, look for the specific region you will work in and click on the **PDF option** for detailed area information if available, or if not, on **Other BLS Products**.
>
> For example, for Washington State, click on the **PDF** for **Seattle Area Economic Activity** or **Other BLS Products** to open a webpage with current information on employment, unemployment, wages, prices, spending and benefits.
>
> The webpage with this information can be found at the bls.gov website address: https://www.bls.gov/regions/economic-summaries.htm#MT.

Record your information of interest for up to TWO states in the table below and on the next page.

1. State____

Region of Interest or Title of Report:	Record Any Information of Interest Below:

2. State____	
Region of Interest or Title of Report:	Record Any Information of Interest Below:

EXCELLENT WORK! 😊

You are now familiar with how to search for an occupational interest in the fastest growing industries (even if there was not specific information readily available about your state), as well as current State and Local employment trends.

In the next section, we will explore how to locate similar occupations across different industries. This will allow us to expand our work options to include other subject areas or fields of knowledge we might like to learn more about, while continuing to do the work we love.

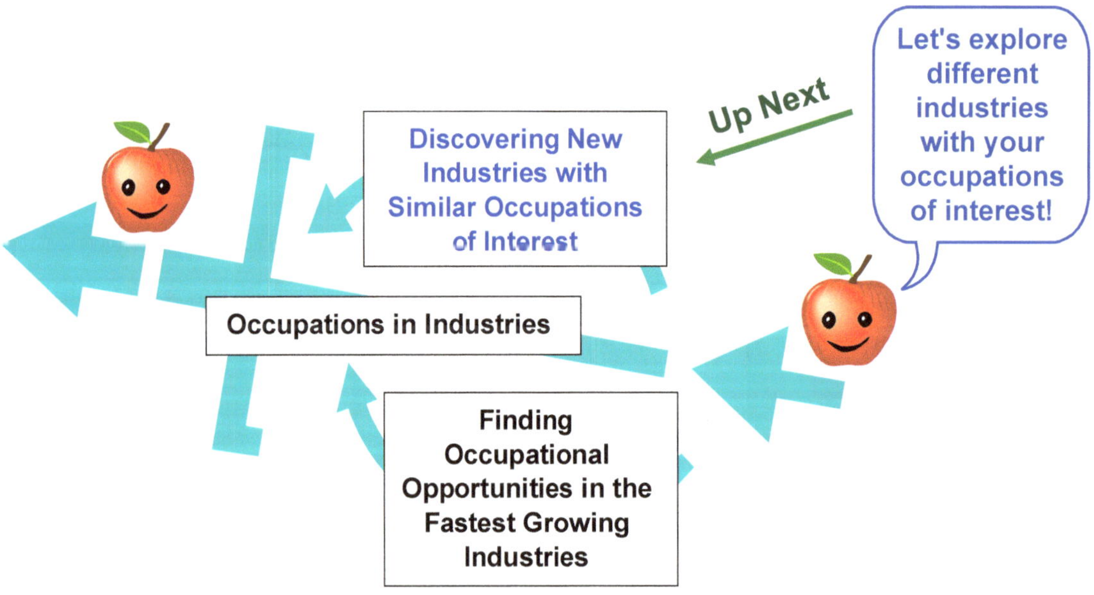

Ready for a break before moving into the next section?

When you are ready, please begin the next page of this Discovery-Guide.

C. DISCOVERY TOOLS 12A-12B – Other Industries with Similar Occupations

One of the advantages when exploring different industries is we have the opportunity to ask ourselves, what other areas of knowledge might we enjoy learning about? When we think for a moment about any type of work – whether in transportation, education, utilities or some other industry – working in a specific industry also informs us more about the knowledge-base or subject areas involved. Ever wanted to know more about a subject area you find interesting? Focusing on finding work in an industry of interest can help us engage a new learning passion as well. For this reason, we will be exploring different and potentially new industries for you to consider in this section of the Discovery-Guide.

Again, we will be utilizing information from different websites, so be sure to follow with the flow-chart and record the information you are gathering in the Discovery Tools as we move along.

1. Go to https://www.mynextmove.org.

2. In the middle of this webpage, look for the center box with the words **Browse careers by industry**.

3. Under **Browse careers by industry** is a box with the words **Administration and Support Services**. Just to the right of this will be an arrow. When you **click on this arrow**, a list of options will be presented.

   Click on one of the industries you are interested in, select the arrow icon to the right of the box and this will take you to a new webpage.

4. This next webpage entitled **Careers in, followed by the industry you selected,** provides a list of different occupations. This list identifies the types of occupations or careers **Most People** or **Some People** have, within this industry.

5. The **Discovery Tools 12A -12B** on the next pages of this Discovery-Guide provide tables for you to record information for TWO of the industries you explore and their corresponding occupational careers. **Select your FIRST Industry, of TWO possible industry explorations**, from the list on the webpage and record your information on the next page of this Discovery-Guide.

1. *Discovery 12A: NEW INDUSTRY EXPLORATION #1*

   Record your information of interest for ONE industry and the corresponding occupational career(s) of interest.

a. **Industry Title** Write in the industry title near the top of the webpage, listed just under **Careers in**.	
b. **Career or Occupational Title(s) Most People or Some People Have.** Write as many Careers or Occupations of Interest in the list on this webpage of **Careers in**.	
c. **Occupational Title and Also called:** **Select at least one occupational career** from the list on the **Careers in** webpage and write in the title. On the webpage with information about your selection, look directly under the career title at the top of the webpage for **Also called** (on the left under the video picture) to locate related job titles.	Occupational Title Selected: Also called:
d. **Additional Information:** (We will be moving to **onetonline.org** after the next Discovery tool for more detailed occupational information.) Knowledge Skills Abilities Personality Technology Education Job Outlook Explore More	

2. *Discovery 12B: NEW INDUSTRY EXPLORATION #2*

Record your information of interest for another industry and corresponding occupational career by returning to the previous webpage or click on **MY NEXT MOVE** at the top of the webpage. Select another option under **Browse careers by industry**. Click on Browse.

a. **Industry Title** Write in the **Industry Title** you are exploring. (This is listed under **Careers in**, near the top of the webpage.)	
b. **Career or Occupational Title(s) Most People or Some People Have.** On the webpage for **Careers in**, write as many Careers or Occupations of Interest in the list.	
c. **Occupational Title and Also Called** Select another occupational career from the list on the **Careers in** webpage and write in the title. Look directly under the career title at the top of the webpage for **Also called** (on the left under the video picture) to locate related job titles.	Occupational Title Selected: Also called:
d. **Additional Information:** (We will be moving to **onetonline.org** in the next section of this Discovery-Guide for more detailed occupational information.) Knowledge Skills Abilities Personality Technology Education Job Outlook Explore More	

EXCELLENT! GREAT WORK! 😊

Next, we will be returning to **onetonline.org** where you will be able to further explore and record information for up to three occupations, from the industries you identified in the Discovery Tools on the previous two pages.

If you still have a webpage open showing a specific occupational career you selected at mynextmove.org, near the bottom of this webpage is the option **See more details at O*NET OnLine**. Clicking on this will bring you directly to the **onetonline.org** webpage with more detailed information about this occupation. The **Discovery Tools 13A-13C** on the next pages of this Discovery-Guide have tables for you to record your information of interest.

To begin at the **onetonline.org** homepage and explore in more detail the industry occupational careers you are interested in, follow along with the flow-chart below.

D. DISCOVERY TOOLS 13A-13C – A More In-Depth Look at Occupations in Different Industries

> 1. Go to https://www.onetonline.org.

> 2. In the "**Occupational keyword search**" box on the upper right side of the webpage, **type in one of your occupational careers of interest** from page 82 or 83 of this Discovery-Guide. Click on **Go**.

> 3. After typing in an occupation and selecting **Go**, you will be taken to a new webpage with detailed information. Continue to the next pages of this Discovery-Guide to record any information of interest in the tables provided.

> 4. After you have finished reviewing the first occupation, return to step #2 above in this flow-chart to explore your second occupation from page 82 or 83, and then a third occupation of interest.

> 5. If any of the occupational careers you are interested in require training, or if you are interested in occupation-related training, guidance will be provided in the next section of this Discovery-Guide when we look for related job postings.

Discovery Tools 13A-13C are on the next pages to record information for up to THREE possible new industry occupations.

1. *Discovery 13A: NEW INDUSTRY OCCUPATION #1*

In the table below, record your information of interest for ONE of the occupational careers you selected on pages 82-83 of this Discovery-Guide.

Title of Industry #1: ____	
Title of Occupation #1: ____	
SOC Code:___________________	Relevant Information and Notes:
• **Sample of Reported Job Titles** • Tasks • Technology Skills • Work Activities • Detailed Work Activities • Work Context • Job Zone • Training & Credentials • Apprenticeship Opportunities • **Skills** • **Knowledge** • Education • **Abilities** • Interests • Work Values • Work Styles • **Wage and Employment Trends** • **Job Openings on the Web** • Related Occupations Additional Information	

2. *Discovery 13B: NEW INDUSTRY OCCUPATION #2*

In the table below, record information for a SECOND occupational interest from pages 82-83 of this Discovery-Guide. (For guidance, return to flow-chart Step #2 on page 84 of this Discovery-Guide.)

Title of Industry #2:____

Title of Occupation #2:____

SOC Code:___________________	Relevant Information and Notes:
• **Sample of Reported Job Titles** • Tasks • Technology Skills • Work Activities • Detailed Work Activities • Work Context • Job Zone • Training & Credentials • Apprenticeship Opportunities • **Skills** • **Knowledge** • Education • **Abilities** • Interests • Work Values • Work Styles • **Wage and Employment Trends** • **Job Openings on the Web** • Related Occupations Additional Information	

3. *Discovery 13C: ADDITIONAL OCCUPATION OF INTEREST #3*

You can record information for any other occupation of interest below, as this will be our final occupational exploration.

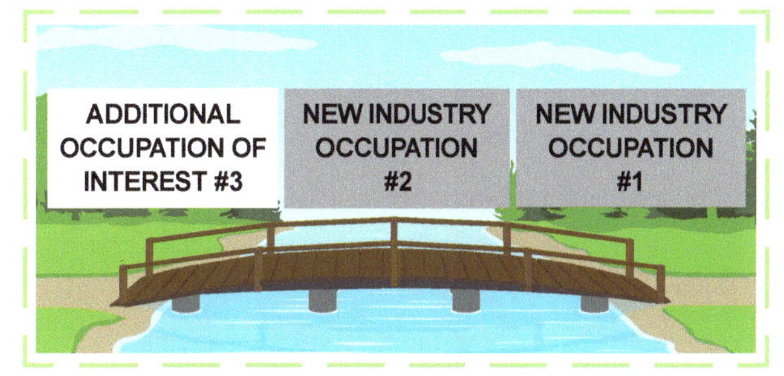

Title of Industry #3:____

Title of Occupation #3:____

SOC Code:____________________	Relevant Information and Notes:
• **Sample of Reported Job Titles** • Tasks • Technology Skills • Work Activities • Detailed Work Activities • Work Context • Job Zone • Training & Credentials • Apprenticeship Opportunities • **Skills** • **Knowledge** • Education • **Abilities** • Interests • Work Values • Work Styles • **Wage and Employment Trends** • **Job Openings on the Web** • Related Occupations Additional Information	

WOW! CONGRATULATIONS! YOU HAVE NOW COMPLETED THE OCCUPATIONAL
EXPLORATIONS IN THIS DISCOVERY-GUIDE!! 😊

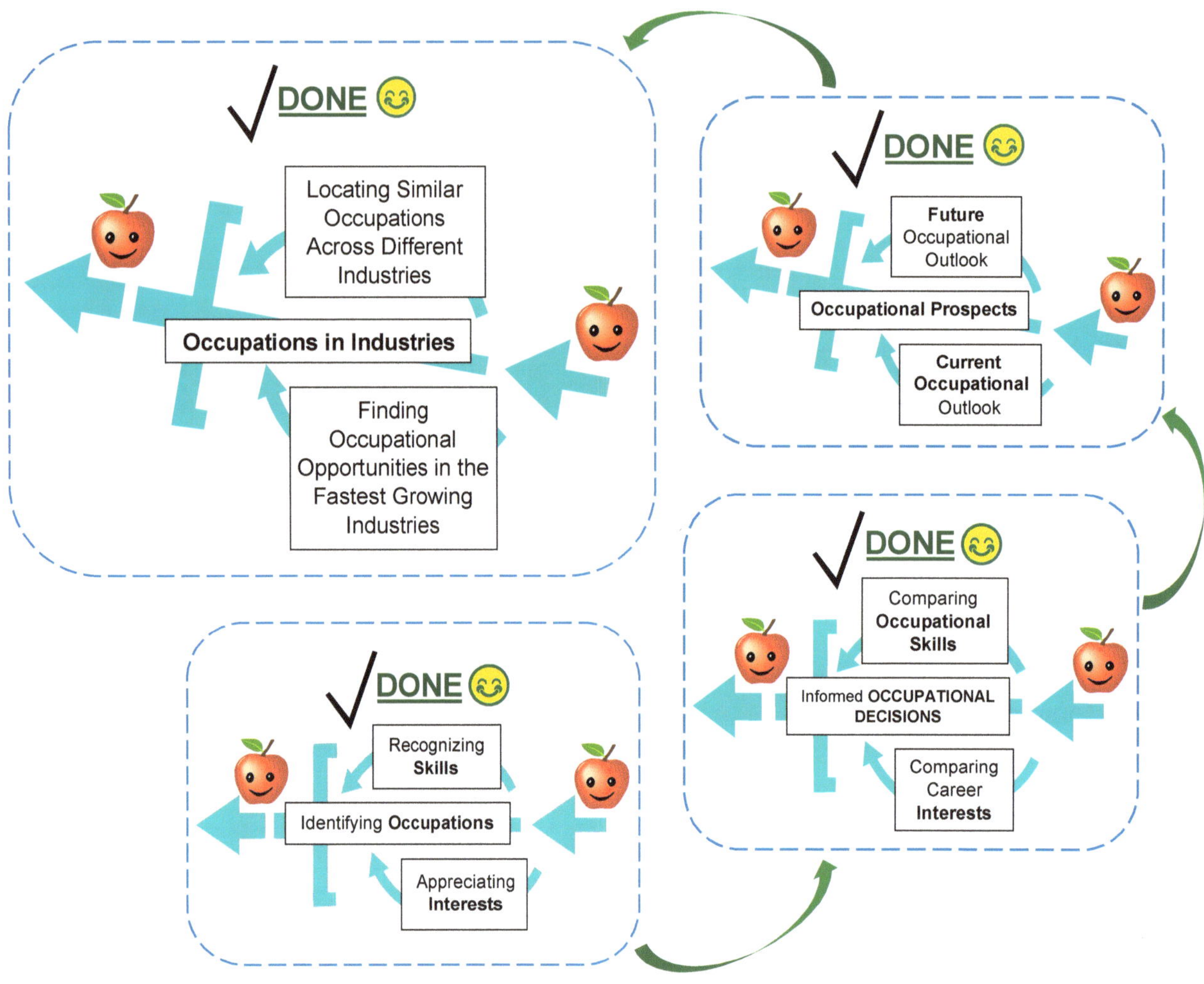

E. Transitioning into Investigating Job Postings

In the final section of this Discovery-Guide, we will turn our attention to utilizing the many
occupations you have identified and organize ourselves for locating actual job postings.
Before we begin this final set of Discovery Tools, let's first review your most relevant
occupations from all of the activities you have worked on throughout this Discovery-Guide.
By having an inventory of your relevant occupational titles, you can engage in a more
focused approach while investigating current job postings.

1. *Discovery 14: ORGANIZING FOR YOUR JOB SEARCH ACTIVITY*

Return to the beginning of this Discovery-Guide and enter into the table below (and continued on the next page), up to SIX different occupations, related industries, related job titles and/or training interests you would like to use when looking for work or training. **We will add current, local wage information from the flow-chart activity ahead on page 91 of this Discovery-Guide.**

Occupation of Interest or Occupational Title	Related Industry or Industries	Reported Job Titles AND/OR Types of Training Required
1.		
SOC Code (if available)	Current Wage and/or Salary Information	
2.		
SOC Code (if available)	Current Wage and/or Salary Information	
3.		
SOC Code (if available)	Current Wage and/or Salary Information	

Occupation of Interest or Occupational Title	Related Industry or Industries	Reported Job Titles AND/OR Types of Training Required
4.		
SOC Code (if available)	Current Wage and/or Salary Information	
5.		
SOC Code (if available)	Current Wage and/or Salary Information	
6.		
SOC Code (if available)	Current Wage and/or Salary Information	
7.		
SOC Code (if available)	Current Wage and/or Salary Information	

Great Work!

With your list of occupations and related titles to use when looking for job postings, you might find wage information tailored to your geographic region useful as well.

Next, we will investigate wage information specific to the State or region you will be job searching in. This information can be added into the table above.

Follow the flow-chart on the next page to locate current, local, wage information.

<table>
<tr><td align="center">For Washington State</td><td></td><td align="center">For Other States and Counties</td></tr>
</table>

For Washington State

1a. Go to https://www.esd.wa.gov/labormarketinfo/occupations or,

at https://www.esd.wa.gov website:

- Select the Labor Market Info option near the top of the webpage.

- On the next webpage, look to the left side for **Employment** and under this, select Occupations (OES). Or, do a search for Employment OEWS.

1b. On the webpage entitled **Occupational employment and wage statistics** (OEWS), scroll down to the table with **Occupational and Employment Wages** to see the most recently available wages by occupation.

1c. You can also locate specific wage information under the headings:

- **Select area(s)** for Washington or click on the arrow for a specific region.

- **Select Occupation** by clicking on the arrow to find your occupation of interest.

OR

For Other States and Counties

2a. Do an internet search for **Occupational Employment and Wage Statistics (OEWS)** or **Occupational Employment Statistics (OES)** and the **State** you would like this information for.

The search should provide results to an official State website with Labor Market Information at a .gov extension.

2b. If you cannot find a .gov website for your State with OEWS or OES information, try calling the State Unemployment office and ask for the website address.

If you are able to find this information, check to see if there are options to compare different geographic areas for your State of interest.

2c. If you are able to locate your occupation of interest, look for the most recent listing of current wages or salaries.

Record your wage information of interest (average, median, wage range) in the table on the previous two pages of this Discovery-Guide. For Washington State information, the 25th and 75th percentile columns identify an hourly wage range for the middle 50% of workers (above 25% and below 75%, for each specific occupation).

EXCELLENT! If you would like to enjoy a moment to appreciate your efforts before moving into the final set of Discovery Tools, now might be a great time! 😊

If we consider the many different Discovery Tools throughout this Discovery-Guide, the intent has been to help us appreciate ourselves and see more clearly how we are so much more than a job(!). We have our life-experiences-to-date and the different kinds of skills we employ regularly or would like to improve upon. We also have interests inspiring us to learn more, and values we seek to live by. Being aware of qualities such as these informs us about who we are, at this moment in time. By acknowledging who we are when looking for work, we support ourselves by being aware and able to articulate what sparks our interests and learning passions.

Whether we find ourselves in the current situation of looking for a survival, gap or target job (as described on pages 7-8), finding the type of work we want to do is important since most WORKER-Seekers (employers) want to hire individuals who love the work they do – whether this involves working with the public, attention to detail, the ability to coordinate efforts as a team, or autonomously completing tasks with minimal supervision. As WORK-Seekers, if we are aware of our interests, skills and learning passions, we are in a better position to discover the best possible working "fit" for us, rather than find ourselves trying to convince a WORKER-Seeker we are a good "fit" for a job we don't really want.

Rather than try to convince a WORKER-Seeker about who we are, we can instead consider sharing what we know about ourselves – our interests, skills and perhaps even future objectives – and ask questions about the work we are interested in, to determine for ourselves if this is a constructive "fit" for us and a potential employer. And, whenever we take the risk to share how we think about our interests and skills, we are learning and becoming more informed by preparing ourselves to engage future situations more effectively and meaningfully.

Although we cannot control when jobs are scarce, when industries decline, or when the economy is incredibly stressed, we can engage in multiple ways to explore different occupations and industries. There may even come a time when our work interests change, and should this occur, re-doing the Discovery Tools in this Discovery-Guide can again help to identify new options and opportunities.

As we move into identifying potential jobs to apply for, keep in mind this will continue to be a process of discovery. Accessing your full scope of work options in your job search activity may require experimenting with different occupations, the different reported job titles linked with specific occupations (as identified at websites like onetonline.org), and considering alternative industries. In addition to the suggested job search approach outlined in this section of the Discovery-Guide, checking into geographically-specific job postings from local newspapers, other local job websites, websites for companies or employers you are interested in, as well as speaking with people you know, can also expand your job search resources.

Finding a job we want to have does take effort and an investment-of-self in terms of time, energy and thoughtful thinking. You can probably identify additional necessary self-efforts as well. Fortunately, we rarely invest our efforts without becoming a better person afterwards, although the benefits we gain may not always manifest in the way, or at the time, we expect. However, even if no one else notices our job search efforts, we can appreciate this inside ourselves and sometimes, this will need to be enough. The constructive efforts we make in our job search will help us continue to fortify our journey with positive resilience too.

As we move into our next Discovery Tool, there are different navigational explanations throughout the flow-chart guides, so reading ahead before studying a job posting will be useful.

When you are ready, let's engage the next part of our journey and explore job postings! 

If you are looking for information on **Training and Certification Resources** instead of jobs, you can move ahead to the next section **B. Locating Potential Training and Certification Resources** on page 101 of this Discovery-Guide.

A. Exploring Job Postings

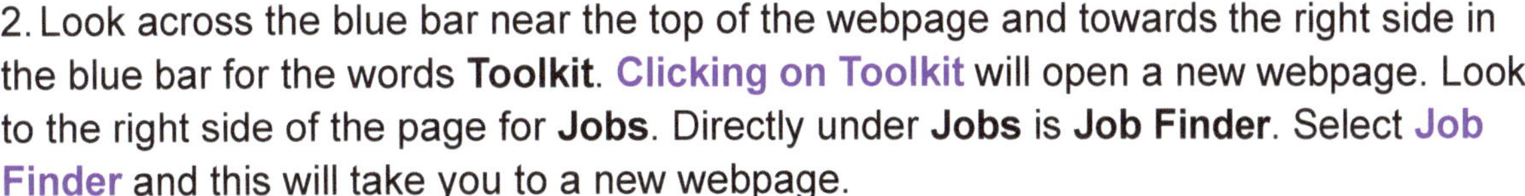

1. Go to https://www.careeronestop.org.

2. Look across the blue bar near the top of the webpage and towards the right side in the blue bar for the words **Toolkit**. **Clicking on Toolkit** will open a new webpage. Look to the right side of the page for **Jobs**. Directly under **Jobs** is **Job Finder**. Select **Job Finder** and this will take you to a new webpage.

3. On the **Job Finder** webpage, look to the left side for **About this data.** Under this heading is an explanation about how the job postings in this search engine support access to two different resources (where the job postings are vetted, as much as possible): **NLx** and **ZipRecruiter**. This means, for example, going directly to these websites will likely duplicate any job searches you initiate at careeronestop.org.

4. On the careeronestop.org Job Finder webpage, look for the box with **Job?** and below this where the **Keyword** box is. **Type in one of the occupations** you listed on pages 89-90 of this Discovery-Guide and move to the next step in this flow-chart.

5. Next to **Job?** is the word **Where?** In the box for **City, State or ZIP code**, **enter the city, state or ZIP code** where you are looking for work.

AN IMPORTANT CONSIDERATION: On your first try, enter the city, state or ZIP code for the preferred area where you want to work. Many people have done broader geographic searches to later learn they are not able to travel as far as they thought they could, without unacceptable hardship.

6. After entering in an occupation and your preferred geographic location, click on **See Jobs** and this will take you to new webpage.

IMPORTANT TO NOTE: Look to the left side of this webpage for the Your Job Search box. This will list the information you entered for Job? and Where?. Below this is Source. This is where you can select your job search source as NLx or ZipRecruiter. Only one of these sources are used in each search.

7. If you do not find enough relevant job postings, or want to search for other similar job postings, you can change the job search **Source** (in the left box entitled **Your Job Search**) and/or the occupation or reported job title as listed on pages 89-90 of this Discovery-Guide, to see if this yields more or different results. (**A reminder: Both careeronestop.org and onetonline.org have reported job titles listed for every occupation.**)

8. Initially, there are 10 job postings listed per webpage and this number can be increased up to 500 per webpage. Look near the bottom of this job postings webpage for **10 per page. Click on the arrow next to the 10** and select a different number to increase the number of job postings per webpage.

9. Clicking on one of the job postings under the words **Job Title** will take you to information about this job. If you receive a pop-up window asking for your email address, you can enter this in, or click in the larger window to remove the pop-up and continue. Information can be recorded on the next page of this Discovery-Guide. You can email, download and save or print the actual posting, or list of jobs, by following the next steps in this flow-chart. If you have your cover letter and resume ready, there is also an option to Apply at the top and bottom of a job post description or you can return to this later, when you have your information ready to submit.

10. To **EMAIL** a copy, if this option is available, look for the envelope icon above the job post (or Job Title) and to the right of the printer icon. Click on the envelope icon to email yourself a copy of the webpage you are looking at.

11. To **DOWNLOAD** and **SAVE**, if available, look near the bottom right side of the webpage for the word **DOWNLOAD**. Clicking on this will provide the option to select the type of file to save as an Excel, PDF, Word or RTF file. Choose the type of file and save to your computer or USB by selecting Submit.

12. To **PRINT** a job posting, look for the printer icon above the job title (or list of postings), next to the envelope icon, and click on this. Or, print using your browser's option.

13. Record your information of interest for up to fourteen jobs in the Discovery Tool 15A beginning on the next page of this Discovery-Guide.

14. Remember you can change the job search engine by selecting a different Source in the box entitled **Your Job Search** on the left side of the webpage.

15. To look for jobs with a different occupational title, return to pages 89-90 of this Discovery-Guide and select a different occupational title to investigate. On the left side of the webpage in the **Your Job Search** box, type another occupation into the **Your Job Search** box under **Jobs?**. Enter the geographic area for your search, select the search engine **Source**, click on See Jobs, and explore more jobs.

If you have adventured off onto different webpages, you can return to step #2 of this flow-chart to start a new search on the **Job Finder** webpage, or if available, click on New Search near the top left side of a webpage.

Turn to the next page of this Discovery-Guide for Discovery Tool 15A to record your job search information.

Guidance for identifying and locating **Training and Certification Resources** begins on page 101 of this Discovery-Guide and your training information of interest can be recorded in Discovery Tool 15B.

1. Discovery 15A: IDENTIFYING JOBS TO APPLY FOR

Record information below and on the next pages to identify, keep track and continue to work on your job finding explorations. 😊

1

Job Search **Source** and Today's Date	Title for Job Post	Company and Website (if listed)
Date Posted and Date Closing		Additional Information: Relevant information? Application submitted?

2

Job Search **Source** and Today's Date	Title for Job Post	Company and Website (if listed)
Date Posted and Date Closing		Additional Information: Relevant information? Application submitted?

3

Job Search **Source** and Today's Date	Title for Job Post	Company and Website (if listed)
Date Posted and Date Closing		Additional Information: Relevant information? Application submitted?

Job Search **Source** and Today's Date	Title for Job Post	Company and Website (if listed)

Date Posted and Date Closing	Additional Information: Relevant information? Application submitted?

Job Search **Source** and Today's Date	Title for Job Post	Company and Website (if listed)

Date Posted and Date Closing	Additional Information: Relevant information? Application submitted?

Job Search **Source** and Today's Date	Title for Job Post	Company and Website (if listed)

Date Posted and Date Closing	Additional Information: Relevant information? Application submitted?

<table>
<tr><td colspan="2">**7**</td></tr>
<tr><td>Job Search **Source** and Today's Date</td><td>Title for Job Post</td><td>Company and Website (if listed)</td></tr>
<tr><td></td><td></td><td></td></tr>
<tr><td colspan="2">Date Posted and Date Closing</td><td>Additional Information: Relevant information? Application submitted?</td></tr>
<tr><td></td><td></td><td></td></tr>
</table>

<table>
<tr><td colspan="2">**8**</td></tr>
<tr><td>Job Search **Source** and Today's Date</td><td>Title for Job Post</td><td>Company and Website (if listed)</td></tr>
<tr><td></td><td></td><td></td></tr>
<tr><td colspan="2">Date Posted and Date Closing</td><td>Additional Information: Relevant information? Application submitted?</td></tr>
<tr><td></td><td></td><td></td></tr>
</table>

<table>
<tr><td colspan="2">**9**</td></tr>
<tr><td>Job Search **Source** and Today's Date</td><td>Title for Job Post</td><td>Company and Website (if listed)</td></tr>
<tr><td></td><td></td><td></td></tr>
<tr><td colspan="2">Date Posted and Date Closing</td><td>Additional Information: Relevant information? Application submitted?</td></tr>
<tr><td></td><td></td><td></td></tr>
</table>

Job Search **Source** and Today's Date	Title for Job Post	Company and Website (if listed)

Date Posted and Date Closing	Additional Information: Relevant information? Application submitted?

Job Search **Source** and Today's Date	Title for Job Post	Company and Website (if listed)

Date Posted and Date Closing	Additional Information: Relevant information? Application submitted?

Job Search **Source** and Today's Date	Title for Job Post	Company and Website (if listed)

Date Posted and Date Closing	Additional Information: Relevant information? Application submitted?

Job Search **Source** and Today's Date	Title for Job Post	Company and Website (if listed)

Date Posted and Date Closing	Additional Information: Relevant information? Application submitted?

Job Search **Source** and Today's Date	Title for Job Post	Company and Website (if listed)

Date Posted and Date Closing	Additional Information: Relevant information? Application submitted?

CONGRATULATIONS ON YOUR GREAT EFFORTS!

Thoughtful exploration and investigation are exactly how we find the kinds of jobs we want to have, and now, you are even more familiar with an approach to support all you have to offer a potential WORKER-Seeker! Terrific!

If you are interested in training or certification information, go to the next page.

If you are not interested in looking into training or certification, move to page 106 of this Discovery-Guide.

B. Locating Potential Training and Certification Resources

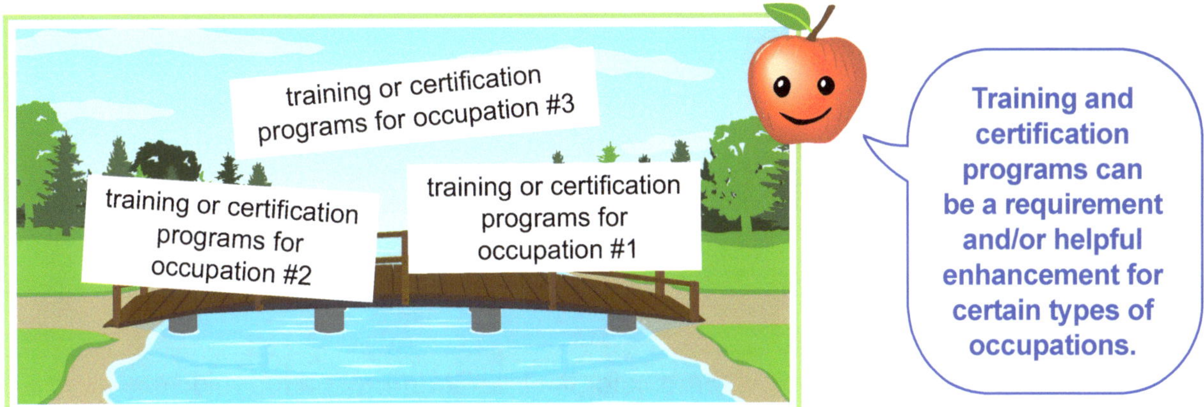

For information on training and certification resources, follow along with the flow-chart provided on the following pages. This is how we shall begin identifying relevant places to investigate training and certification opportunities to support our occupational interests.

Training and certifications courses can be pre-requisites, or helpful knowledge-building enhancements for certain types of occupations, such as training to be a medical assistant or receiving certification for work as a program manager. Enrolling in these types of programs, which can range from a few months to a few years, usually offers enhanced learning and practical experience to employ in a specific type of work.

Sometimes, financial assistance for a training or certification program is available. All States provide a local Eligible Training Provider List (ETPL) which identifies government-funded financial assistance for training and sometimes, certification programs as well. The funding available is designed to incentivize and support high-growth or in-demand occupations.

> To find the Eligible Training Provider List (ETPL) for your State, do an internet search with the words **eligible training provider list** or **ETPL** and **the State** you are interested in. For example, **ETPL Washington State** will provide search results to a Washington State government website, where you can navigate through to locate this state's ETPL. The same type of results will occur for searches with other states.

In addition, One-Stop centers (or WorkSource in Washington State) usually have job counselors to assist with identifying potential funding sources to help pay for some of the training and/or certification cost. Contact your state government unemployment agency, a local One-Stop unemployment service center or WorkSource in Washington State, and ask who you can speak with for more information about possible training and certification funding assistance. Of significant importance is to investigate potential funding opportunities **before** committing to a specific training or certification program, as most forms of financial assistance cannot be applied retroactively, after an application and acceptance process has been finalized.

To investigate possible training and certification programs:

1. Go to https://www.careeronestop.org.

2. Look across the dark blue bar near the top of the webpage and click on the word **Toolkit** to move to a new webpage.

3. On the **Toolkit** webpage, look in the box for the title **Training** in a top middle column. Depending on whether you are looking for training or certification, select **Local Training Finder** or **Certification Finder**. This will take you to a new webpage.

4. For:
Local Training Finder

5. For:
Certification Finder

4a. On the **Local Training Finder** webpage, type in an **Occupation, Occupational (SOC) Code, School or Program** you listed on pages 89-90 of this Discovery-Guide. In the adjacent box to the right, type in the **City, State or ZIP Code** to specify the geographic area you want to search. Click on **Search** to receive a list of training places.

5a. On the **Certification Finder** webpage, type in a **Certification Name, Organization, Industry, Occupation or Occupational SOC code** in the box provided from your list on pages 89-90 of this Discovery-Guide. When you are ready, click on **Search** and this will bring you to a list of certification places. **The left side of the webpage may also have a list of Related Occupations, occupations In Demand and/ or a related Industry (or industries). Under the Search box is a List of Occupations and below this, a List of Industries. Click on the + icon to see a general list of occupations or industries.**

Continue to the next page…

6. A table is provided at the end of this flow-chart in **Discovery Tool 15B** for you to record relevant information about potential training and/or certification options.

7. You can **email, print or download and save** the list provided in the **Local Training Finder**. The **Certification Finder** only includes the option to **Download**. However, you can record information in the table provided on the next page of this Discovery-Guide. If relevant, you can also change the number of places listed per webpage (above the **Download** option at the bottom of the webpage) to include the full list.

OR

8. From the **Local Training Finder** you can **email, print or download and save the list** provided.

8. The **Certification Finder** may not have an email, print or download function. If not, **use the tables on the next page to record your information**.

9. To **EMAIL** a list from the Local Training Finder, look for the **envelope icon** above the search on the left side, and to the right of the printer icon. Click on the **envelope icon** to email yourself a copy of the webpage you are looking at.

10. To **PRINT** the list, look for the **printer icon** near the top left and next to the **envelope icon** and click on this.

11. To **DOWNLOAD and SAVE** a list, look just above the bottom of the webpage for the word **Download**. Clicking on this will provide the option to select the type of file to save as **Excel, PDF, Word or RTF**. Choose the type of file you want and save to your computer or USB.

12. **Note: Many of the entries from both the Local Training Finder and the Certification Finder will bring you to the organization's website or provide a website address. If there is information about the length of the program or types of programs, check the organization's website in case program changes have been made, but are not yet reflected in the information provided at careeronestop.org.**

Move to the next page of this Discovery-Guide to record your information of interest on Training and/or Certification programs.

1

School Name and Location OR Certification Name	Website Address
Program Name OR Certifying Organization	Length of Program, Type of Program, Additional Information

2

School Name and Location OR Certification Name	Website Address
Program Name OR Certifying Organization	Length of Program, Type of Program, Additional Information

3

School Name and Location OR Certification Name	Website Address
Program Name OR Certifying Organization	Length of Program, Type of Program, Additional Information

School Name and Location OR Certification Name	Website Address
Program Name OR Certifying Organization	**Length of Program, Type of Program, Additional Information**

School Name and Location OR Certification Name	Website Address
Program Name OR Certifying Organization	**Length of Program, Type of Program, Additional Information**

School Name and Location OR Certification Name	Website Address
Program Name OR Certifying Organization	**Length of Program, Type of Program, Additional Information**

CONGRATULATIONS! GREAT WORK!

AMAZING ACCOMPLISHMENT – YOU HAVE COMPLETED THIS DISCOVERY-GUIDE!! 😊 😊 Whew!

XVII. READY, MORE PREPARED, AND MOVING INTO THE FUTURE

Hopefully, this Discovery-Guide helps you feel more confident and comfortable about knowing where you currently are in this journey we refer to as LIFE. Most importantly, we hope your efforts shall continue to fortify your resilience as we take another step into our future.

Since all of the websites we visited provide material based on Labor Market Information, AMAZINGLY, you are now also more familiar with using Labor Market Information and working with Labor Market Data to assist with your work-life decision-making.

CONGRATULATIONS!

We hope you will revisit the Discovery Tools in this Discovery-Guide whenever you are considering any future work or career transition.

Thank you for sharing your journey with us! 😊

APPENDIX

APPENDIX A:

HOLLAND CODES**

The **Holland Codes**, developed by John Holland (1985), is a system to classify jobs into job categories, interest clusters, or work personality environments. In the Holland Model, these categories represent work personalities.

The work personalities are:

- **Realistic** people are usually assertive and competitive, and are interested in activities requiring motor coordination, skill and strength. People with a realistic orientation usually prefer to work a problem through by doing something, rather than talking about it, or sitting and thinking about it. They like concrete approaches to problem solving, rather than abstract theory. They tend to be interested in scientific or mechanical rather than cultural and aesthetic areas. They like to work with THINGS.

- **Investigative** people like to think and observe rather than act, to organize and understand information rather than to persuade. They tend to prefer individual rather than people-oriented activities. They like to work with DATA.

- **Artistic** people are usually creative, open, inventive, original, perceptive, sensitive, independent and emotional. They do not like structure and rules, enjoy tasks involving people or physical skills, and are more likely to express their emotions than others. They like to think, organize, and understand artistic and cultural areas. They like to work with IDEAS and THINGS.

- **Social** people seem to engage their interests in teaching or helping situations. Different than R and I Types, they are drawn more towards close relationships with other people and less likely to gain as much satisfaction from intellectual or physical tasks. They like to work with PEOPLE.

- **Enterprising** people are good talkers and use this skill to lead or persuade others. They also value reputation, power, money and status, and will usually direct their attention towards these kinds of achievements. They like to work with PEOPLE and DATA.

- **Conventional** people like rules and regulations and emphasize being able to maintain self-control. They like structure and order, and dislike unstructured or unclear work and interpersonal situations. They place value on reputation, power, or status. They like to work with DATA.

Assessments using Holland Personality Styles link vocational interests to job families. Reference: John Holland (1985) Making Vocational Choices (2nd ed.) Odessa, FL.: Psychological Assessment Resources, Inc.

**The information on this page about the Holland Codes was copied from CareerOneStop.org (on a webpage that no longer exists). However, additional information about the Interest Assessment can be found at: https://www.careeronestop.org/Toolkit/Careers/interest-assessment-help.aspx

APPENDIX B

GLOSSARY OF TERMS

Career – "A career spans your lifetime and includes your education, training, professional memberships, volunteering and your full history of paid work."[1]

Dictionary of Occupational Titles (D-O-T) – The Dictionary of Occupational Titles (D-O-T) was created by the Employment and Training Administration to identify occupational titles by corresponding numerical designations and has been replaced by O*NET. More information can be found at: https://www.dol.gov/agencies/oalj/topics/libraries/LIBDOT.

Industry – "An 'industry' describes the collection of companies and organizations connected with producing a particular product or service, such as cars, software, health care, or energy."[2]

Job – "A job is what you show up to work for."[3]

KSAs: Knowledge, Skills and Abilities – KSA(s) is an acronym describing the Knowledge, Skills and Abilities necessary or desired for a specific career and/or job.

North American Industry Classification System or NAICS – A system for classifying the economic activity of industries on the North American continent (Canada, Mexico and the United States) using numerical codes. More information for use in the U.S. can be found at: https://www.census.gov/naics - select the "History" or "FAQs" topic near the top of the webpage for additional information.

Occupation – "An occupation describes a type of work with associated tasks, education and training, typical wages, work setting and more."[4]

Occupational Outlook Handbook (OOH) – This handbook provides information on the duties, education, training, pay and future outlook for occupations and is published by the Department of Labor, Bureau of Labor Statistics.[5] More information is available at: https://www.bls.gov/ooh.

Standard Occupational Classification (SOC) – The Standard Occupational Classification, or SOC, is a classification system based on a federal statistical standard to classify all types of work into numerically organized occupational categories, commonly referred to as SOC codes. More information is available at https://www.bls.gov/soc.

---

[1] https://www.careeronestop.org/Help/FAQs-Explore-Careers.aspx
[2] https://www.careeronestop.org/ExploreCareers/Learn/research-industries.aspx
[3] https://www.careeronestop.org/Help/FAQs-Explore-Careers.aspx
[4] https://www.careeronestop.org/Help/FAQs-Explore-Careers.aspx
[5] https://www.bls.gov/ooh/about/ooh-faqs.htm

APPENDIX C
LABOR MARKET INFORMATION WEBSITES

https://www.bls.gov/ooh: For information from the Occupational Outlook Handbook (OOH) by the Bureau of Labor Statistics.

https://www.careeronestop.org: For information about occupations as potential careers sponsored by the U.S. Department of Labor.

https://www.census.gov/naics: For information about the North American Industry Classification System.

https://www.esd.wa.gov: The official website for Labor Market Information in Washington State from the Washington State Employment Security Department. Look for a menu option on "Labor Market Info" or enter a search for "labor market info" at the esd.wa.gov website.

https://www.mynextmove.org: A CareerOneStop.org website focusing on assisting job seekers and students with information on over 900 different careers. **This is a great place to explore Labor Market Information if you are planning to move to a new geographic location**.

https://www.myskillsmyfuture.org: Developed by the National Center for O*NET Development to help match one's occupational skills and experiences with the same or similar skills utilized in other occupations.

https://www.onetonline.org: For occupational information with extensive descriptions on Knowledge, Skills and Abilities (KSAs) to assist with resume writing and other occupation-related research. Sponsored by the U.S. Department of Labor.

* https://www.worksourcewa.com: The official website for WorkSource centers (a partnership of state, local and nonprofit agencies) in Washington State assisting with job and career tools, schedules for training, events, workshops and other job search and employer resources.

> *** Each state in the U.S. should have a similar website, although the name of the agency might be different. To find the website, try doing a search for the State you are interested in, followed by WorkSource or One-Stop Career Center. Look for a .gov extension for additional resources within a specific state.**

Acknowledgements*

To Bill Gore, Ph.D., for his unwavering dedication to mentoring, exuberant belief in the creative intellect, for his many years of companionship and sharing of wisdom, and his insistence I publish to share my perspective with others, which I am finally doing. While I miss our many heartfelt discussions about society (and its discontents), I remember those special times with much affection and admiration. May he rest in peace.

To Werner Schimmelbusch, M.D., who has faithfully guided me towards an understanding and engagement of the human experience and the (developmental) cycles we all live through across our lifetimes in a manner filled with empathy, grace and dignity. I am truly grateful for his sharing of acquired wisdom so I might utilize an applied psychoanalytic approach to support the resilience and hope of others, such as through this Discovery-Guide.

A very appreciative "Thank You!" to all the workshop participants and intrepid individuals working through this Discovery-Guide (and its previous versions). Your insights, constructive suggestions, humorous enjoyment from learning and your willingness to explore a different approach made this Discovery-Guide experience a joy to work on and improve.

A heartfelt "Thank You!" to Albert Garza, Administrator (WorkSource Auburn and Temporarily at WorkSource Rainier), Washington Employment Security Department*, for his effective support from the very beginning with masterfully orchestrating trial workshops, feedback from job counselors, and follow-up interviews. His dedication to improving the lives of others helped us polish this Discovery-Guide to work for a wide range of diverse individuals.

A special "Thank you!" to Anneliese Vance-Sherman, Regional Labor Economist, Washington Employment Security Department*, for her open invitation to sharing her considerable professional acumen. Her expert knowledge of Labor Market Information strategies has made this Discovery-Guide much more useful than would have otherwise been possible.

Much appreciation to Brad McGuire, former WorkSource Integration Manager, King County Department of Community and Human Services*, for his earnest commitment and enthusiasm with moving this Discovery-Guide into a set of initial workshop trials with job counselors, which provided the opportunity for us to listen and learn from those working to help others find the work they want to do.

*Please note: The intent of these acknowledgments is to recognize those individuals instrumental with helping us improve and polish this Discovery-Guide. This does not represent an endorsement by any agency or organizational entity.

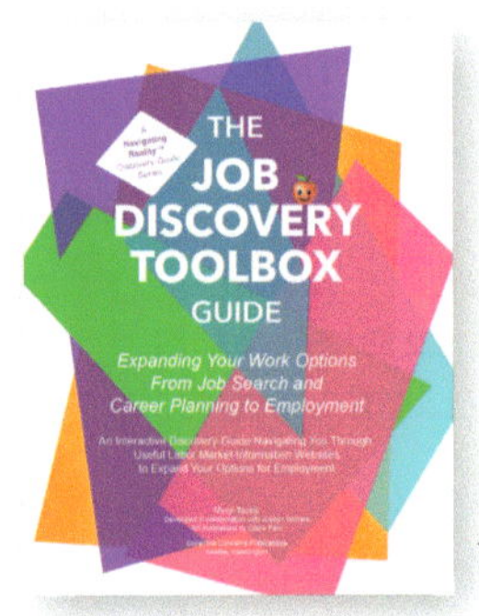

The Job Discovery Toolbox Guide

A comprehensive and interactive job and career Discovery-Guide with tools to help identify your strengths, expand job opportunities and explore career paths. Whether you're a job seeker, a career changer or simply looking to enhance your professional skills, this Discovery-Guide is a useful and practical approach to finding the work you want to do. Paperback and digital PDF available. A spiral bound will be available soon - check https://www.navigatingreality.com under Learning Tools for more information.

The Job Discovery Toolbox Guide - Special Editions

Customizable book cover for organizations and organizational workshops.

COMING OCTOBER 2024:

Introducing Our New Series Beginning July 2024: A **Navigating Reality™** for Kids Series with our first story, **Yuki the Magical Dog**

Join Yuki as she learns to navigate her world and share her happiness magic to help others. Follow along as her happiness magic grows with her, and discover what she learns along the way.

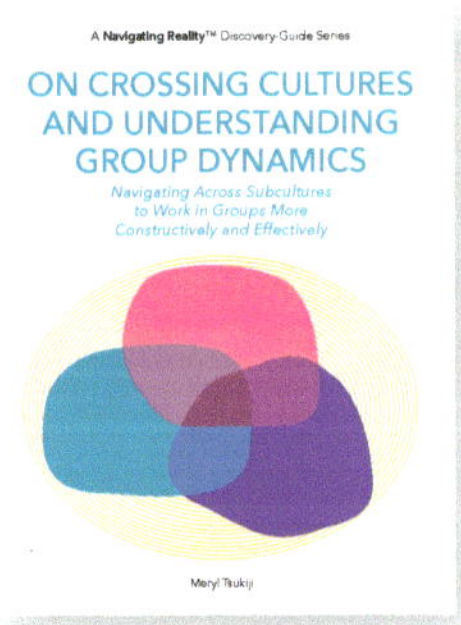

The next addition to our Navigating Reality™ Discovery-Guide Series:

On Crossing Cultures and Understanding Group Dynamics

An interactive guide to help understand how personal life experiences in different subcultures, such as family, friends, workplace, school, etc., influence different individual approaches and interactions in group-based collaboration.